10/13

8.95

Adelaide

Other titles in this series
In Search of Hobart by Peter Timms, with an introduction
    by Robert Dessaix
Brisbane by Matthew Condon
Sydney by Delia Falconer
Melbourne by Sophie Cunningham

Forthcoming
Canberra by Paul Daley

Adelaide

KERRYN GOLDSWORTHY

NEWSOUTH

A NewSouth book

Published by
NewSouth Publishing
University of New South Wales Press Ltd
University of New South Wales
Sydney NSW 2052
AUSTRALIA
www.newsouthpublishing.com.au

© Kerryn Goldsworthy 2011
First published 2011

This book is copyright. Apart from any fair dealing for the purpose
of private study, research, criticism or review, as permitted under the
Copyright Act, no part may be reproduced by any process without
written permission. Inquiries should be addressed to the publisher.

National Library of Australia
Cataloguing-in-Publication entry
  Author: Goldsworthy, Kerryn.
  Title: Adelaide / by Kerryn Goldsworthy.
  ISBN: 978 174223 262 1 (hbk.)
  Series: Cities series.
  Subjects: Adelaide (S. Aust.) – History.
            Adelaide (S. Aust.) – Social life and customs.
            Adelaide (S. Aust.) – Biography.
  Dewey Number: 994.231

Design Josephine Pajor-Markus
Cover Sandy Cull, gogoGingko
Cover photo Kerryn Goldsworthy
Endpaper map David Atkinson, handmademaps.com
Printer Everbest

This book is printed on paper using fibre supplied from plantation
or sustainably managed forests.

Contents

'When you live in a place you learn all the stories of that place.'

— Uncle Lewis Yerloburka O'Brien

I
Introduction:
Contradictions

Queen Adelaide, the consort of King William IV and the person for whom Adelaide was named, was a German princess who had been christened Amalie Adelheid Louise Therese Karolina Wilhelmina, and was known as the Princess Adelheid. To help the struggling lacemakers of England after she became its Queen, she ordered from them a Honiton lace gown embroidered round the hem with flowers the initials of whose names spelt out her own, the anglicised 'Adelaide': Amaranth, Daphne, Eglantine, Lilac, Auricula, Ivy, Dahlia, and Eglantine again.

But had she wanted this pretty picture-puzzle gown to tell her true name, she would have had to unpick the last four flowers and re-arrange and re-stitch them, substituting for the auricula a stem of hollyhocks, or a sprig of heather, or a spray of heart's-ease. And even then, it could be argued that what was really required was a pattern of Amaranth, Mimosa, Alyssum, Lilac, Ivy and Eglantine. The story of Adelaide is ornamented with ambiguities and ironies small and large; even its name is not quite what it seems, and we could easily have been called Amalie instead.

Many of the myths, legends, received opinions and oft-repeated staples of public memory about the city have been, or could be, challenged. The Adelaide climate, for example, has been habitually described as 'Mediterranean', but bears only a sketchy resemblance to the Mediterranean of our experience and dreams. The Aboriginal people of the Adelaide Plains have been widely known to South Australians as the Kaurna since Norman Tindale published *Aboriginal Tribes of Australia* in 1974, but it's now thought that his classification may be a little over-simple and misleading. Much has been made of Adelaide's pride in its convict-free origins, but the state's two main founding fathers, Edward Gibbon Wakefield and Robert Gouger, both spent time in prison. The date on which the first Governor arrived in South Australia and proclaimed it a colony, 28 December 1836, is remembered as the birth of South Australia and celebrated by a public holiday called Proclamation Day, but South Australia's 'real' birthday was 19 February of that year, when the British Government issued the Letters Patent that brought the Province of South Australia into being as a geopolitical reality. Far from embracing the ideals of 'systematic colonisation' claimed by the founding fathers, many wealthy Britons were induced to buy land in the new colony by assurances that investment in South Australia would be money for jam. Colonel William Light is one of Adelaide's heroes, traditionally credited with choosing the site and designing the layout of Adelaide, but some historians in recent decades have argued that most of – if not all – the credit should really go to his deputy, George Kingston. And even if they are wrong, the site called 'Light's Vision' featuring his statue at the top of Montefiore Hill is not, in fact, the place where Light made his choice of site and began his survey.

In more recent times, the 'Weird Adelaide' tag is most often a reference to the string of disappearances, serial murders and other macabre crimes that have occurred here since the 1960s, but in fact the crime statistics of other Australian cities are much the same. And the label 'City of Churches', sitting most oddly side by side with Adelaide's reputation for macabre sex crimes, is usually invoked to make a point about the piety and rectitude of church-going Adelaideans — by people ignoring the fact that churches, when built, are dedicated to particular denominations, and the number of them in Adelaide attests not so much to a blanket piety as to the heterogeneity of worship and religious freedom that has been a feature of the city from its earliest days. There are five churches within easy walking distance of my house, but they are Slavic Pentecostal, Slavic Evangelical Baptist, common-or-garden Baptist, Seventh Day Adventist and Greek Orthodox. All are well tended and attended, but somehow I don't think it's quite what either those who coined or those who still use the phrase 'City of Churches' had in mind.

Any investigation of Adelaide's history will reveal a tension between two kinds of sense-making operations. There's the never-ending weave of mythmaking by writers and artists, reinforced by the simplifications of journalism and television and the unrecorded workings of collective memory, which is to do with community and belonging and which likes lively stories, obvious heroes, dramatic imagery and clear-cut conflicts in which good triumphs over evil. And then, on the other hand, there's the patient picking apart and re-stitching done by historians, by anthropologists, by ecologists, discovering truths and uncovering untruths as they all continually make and unmake and remake the story of a city, like Penelope patiently unravelling her tapestry at night as she fends off the suitors and waits for Ulysses to come home. This no doubt is true of every city, but somehow it all seems more visible here. More visible, and more extreme.

I've lived in Adelaide for a little less than half my life, but it has always been my city. When I was a child, everyone in my family, like the rest of our small South Australian farming community, referred to Adelaide as 'Town'. The word always had an audible capital, as though 'Town' were Adelaide's real name; from the vantage point of the farm, Town was the archetypal metropolis, the place where all human needs and desires could be met. Town was a place of traffic and bright lights, of department stores, medical specialists, movies, buses, and the newfangled discount supermarkets where you could buy a carload of non-perishable groceries in bulk for a fraction of their country cost: three months' supply of cornflour and cornflakes, washing-up detergent and canned tomatoes, sanitary napkins, shampoo, spaghetti and other untold riches would be crammed into the back of the station wagon for the three-hour drive home. Town meant the paternal grandparents, the orthodontist, the Royal Adelaide Show, the crowded beaches, the buying of shoes and winter clothes. Town was where the sporty kids from school went to compete at higher levels, and where the clever kids went away to do a fifth year of high school as sad but stoic boarders.

I was 12 when my family moved to Town and 26 when I moved on alone to a bigger Town, not in any spirit of escape but rather in quest of adventure, broader horizons and a good working life. I lived and worked in Melbourne for almost two decades, and for all that time, just as it had been before we left the farm, Adelaide was still my point of reference. It wasn't called Town any more; now it was called Home. With a pair of interior compasses like that, there would have been no hope of any kind of objectivity in writing about Adelaide even if that had been my aim. But in any case you can be objective only about cities you've never set foot in, and usually not then either.

Any place you have experienced first-hand is a museum of memory, one whose exhibits conjure up, in widening ripples of association, a whole city: a red paddle-boat, a photograph of three children on a hot day, a marble Venus fetchingly half-naked in the shade. In this book I have made a small collection of objects, most of them well-known public images or landmarks of some kind but a few of them things from my own memory, that seem to me redolent of the city. Most of them recall some aspect of its history, and most of them will have immediate resonance in the minds of people who recognise them, as repositories of meaning and memory. The more private objects – the concert ticket, the bucket of peaches – are the ones that have special meaning for me but also speak of public things, of politics and education and culture.

In one of the most important and influential Australian essays of recent times, David Malouf wrote of Brisbane as 'the only place I know from inside, from my body outwards'. To know a place from your body outwards is to know it from childhood, and to know it most vividly not from books, films, photographs or even maps, but from standing in it, walking in it, driving or singing or playing football or giving birth in it. Perhaps most of all, you get to know a place in a bodily way by falling in it: falling over, falling pregnant, falling in with the wrong crowd, falling in love. This sort of knowledge of a place builds up slowly, an accretion of bodily memories over time, but there's also the kind of knowledge that comes in illuminating flashes: the kind of knowledge of a city that comes from remembering what you saw and heard not just in that spot but also at that moment, determined by the time of day, your state of mind, the way the light fell. In that sense at least, and as with any other place, there is no such thing as 'Adelaide': there are as many Adelaides as there are people who have stood and looked, and listened, and remembered.

Late on a winter's night in 2005, I'm walking back to the car after seeing a play at Adelaide University's Little Theatre. The car is parked in Victoria Drive, the gently winding road along the back of the campus that separates it from the river. It's cold and dark and silent and there's nobody about, and just as I'm thinking what a triumphant moment this would be for those who complain of

Adelaide's smallness and uneventfulness, there's a roaring and whumping noise overhead. I look up to see a helicopter, now deafening and brilliantly lit up, descending to land like a bejewelled dragonfly on the roof of the Royal Adelaide Hospital. In the darkness it's a chaos and drama of noise and bright lights in mid-air, as someone brings someone else to be saved, and lands on the roof of this huge building full of broken, dying or recovering Adelaideans, asleep, or working ones with their clipboards and scalpels, wide awake.

To the right there's the university, with its hum of sleeping books and its occasional rectangle of light in a high window where someone is solving a problem or meeting a deadline or marking a pile of essays, and further along there's the Torrens Parade Ground, where for over a century soldiers have gathered to march away – to the Boer War, World War I, World War II – and where they still gather to reunite, as the Vietnam War Memorial overlooks them from under the trees, set back from the road and starkly lit.

And to the left there's the steep river bank, not, after all, entirely silent, with its faint cluck and lap of water, picturesque even at night with its dim old-fashioned lamps whose light just hints at the flowerbeds and willows beyond in the dark. But this bank is a notorious and long-established gay beat, as well as the longtime haunt of student lovers; the bridge outside the zoo a little way upstream is the scene of some macabre and tragic deaths, and the water a final trap for the many who over the years have fallen, or jumped, or been swept away, or pushed. So much violence and sex and death for such a little river. But then I think of other, bigger rivers, the great rivers in the great cities of the world – of standing on bridges in Vienna or London and looking down into the currents of the Danube or the Thames, into water of a muscular and opaque brown, swirling away the evidence of ancient and not so ancient crimes – and think perhaps that when it comes to violence and sex and death, all rivers in cities are the same.

I get into the car, shivering a bit, and drive in the other direction from the hospital, to the end of Victoria Drive at its T-junction with King William Road. Stopped at the red light, I look southwest through the bare trees to the tall buildings and bright lights of North Terrace, across the broad sweep of the Elder Park lawn as it slopes down to the Torrens Lake. That's a panorama of coloured light on dark water, great folded swathes of blackness relieved by embroideries of light in lines both straight and curved: by the illuminated arcs of river bank and treetop silhouette, the spray of the river fountains as they catch and atomise the light, and the echoes of merry-go-round and circus tent in the lit-up late-Victorian outline of the Rotunda and its music of a century and more. The lights of buildings old and new on the most built-up part of North Terrace shine down into the water, and are reflected back: the lights from the Casino, where people are feeding money to the hungry animals of hope and greed, and from the tall clump of interlocking hexagonal towers that used to be the Hyatt and are now the Intercontinental, its honeycomb cell-rooms packed full of people sleeping, brushing their hair, making love, sending emails, drinking wine, or looking out the window at the flat broad views away to the north, with their straight lines of street lights converging on the black horizon. Yes, it's a small city. But it's dense with daily life, haunted by ghosts and thick with history.

2
The Map

Here is a fold-out map of Adelaide, designed for the use of visitors. You can see the way the city proper sits pleasingly foursquare on the page, geometrically patterned with smaller squares of green inside its grid of streets, oriented to the points of the compass. The original plan of 1837 was more symmetrical, with bigger areas of green; if you compare it with this map you can see where development and traffic management have changed the streets and nibbled away at the edges and corners of the little open parks. But even now, this map with its flowerlike geometry and its delicate black and white lines over cool greens and greys looks like a patterned tile in some grand and ancient house: Greek? Etruscan? Moorish?

To see the city reduced schematically to its straight lines and square corners, the streets running due north–south or east–west, is somehow reassuring in a way that reading the maps of more tangled cities is not. The maps of such Roman Empire cities as Paris or Florence, or of a city like Sydney, whose streets are subservient to the drama of topography, can seem labyrinthine when you are trying to find your way, but planning a route from A to B on the Adelaide map is an easy and pleasant thing, more like negotiating a small piece of tartan cloth. This is something that Melburnians also understand.

North of this grid of streets, the river undulates through the middle of the map, swelling into a recreational lake surrounded by a big open park and setting up a mild sense of visual tension between the straight lines and corners of streets and the leisurely irregular curves of river, park and lake. To the north again, across the wide belts of green on either side of the river, there are three smaller grids of different sizes, intersecting at their corners, cattywumpus to the compass points and clearly laid out to fit the curve of the river and sit easily with the terrain, which is higher and more uneven on the northern side of the river. This is North Adelaide, largely residential but part of the original layout of 1837. 'We were in a country perfectly in a state of nature,' wrote Colonel Light:

and the obstructions for this work were greater on this particular spot than any other part of the plain. It may be asked then 'Why choose it?' I answer, 'Because it was on a beautiful and gently rising ground, and formed altogether a better connection with the river than any other place.'

There's a wide protective border of green, the Parklands, which separates Adelaide and North Adelaide from the suburbs beyond, encircling them both in the shape of a figure 8 with the river at its waist. When it comes to the Parklands, even the most hardened Adelaide realist can and often does turn nature mystic; despite the best efforts of developers over the years, the city has somehow managed to retain most of the original green belt that the first Surveyor-General, the consumptive Colonel Light, wistfully called the lungs of his city. It has shaped the growth of the suburbs beyond in strange ways; unlike most cities that spread imperceptibly outwards from their commercial core to the inner suburbs and thence to the outer suburbs, Adelaide's original design remains encapsulated, separated from its outward sprawl. Inner suburbs like Norwood began as separate villages, and still have their own internal logic and character.

The city proper – the southern grid, which

includes the CBD – is bounded by four broad terraces, with East Terrace staggered to fit the low-
lying ground on that side of the city. Apart from
that, it's symmetrical, but not a regular checker-
board; twice as many streets run east–west as run
north–south, Colonel Light's aim being to protect
the city from the worst of the hot north winds
laden with red dust from the desert. Between East
Terrace and West Terrace there are only three other
north–south streets in Light's original plan; one of
them, King William Street, runs down the centre of
the grid and explains why the cross streets change
their names halfway along – one must never cross
the path of the King. Light could not have antici-
pated the invention of the automobile, or the fact
that if you're driving due west down any of these
streets at the end of a clear hot day, the horizontal
rays from the molten gold of the setting sun are far
too much for any visor or pair of sunglasses, and
westbound city drivers become a danger to themselves and all around them, blinded by the light.

Along the broad old boulevard of North Terrace, with its patches of elegance and swathes of
shade, there are many of the essential institutions
of a city: Parliament House, Government House,
the main city hospital, the railway station, the

convention centre, and most of the bigger hotels. There's also what the Council likes to call the 'cultural precinct', a particularly pretty stretch of the street where the state library, the museum, the art gallery and the University of Adelaide, in that order, sit side by side on the land between the street frontage and the slope down to the river. Beyond the eastern end of North Terrace are the Botanical Gardens; beyond the western end, the paddock where the big gentle police horses can be found quietly conversing under the olive trees, the police barracks across the road, and beyond that the disquieting, Dickensian Old Adelaide Gaol. Historically, North Terrace was — and to a large extent still is — the place you go to be punished, governed, educated or healed.

But while North Terrace has so many of the big institutions of government and culture, it also has little patches and pockets of something else. Young women scantily clad in satiny clothes line up under the golden streetlights and the silver moonlight to get into the nightclubs where bouncers loom like vampires in the shadows. Teenage boys, wiry and restless, descend in large numbers on the little skate park under the Adelaide sun and surge past each other in wild loops around its deadly concrete curves. A little way east, the casino houses the loud and lurid machinery of gambling and the thousands of people searching there for proof that they are loved and favoured by some god or gods, something they once sought across the road in the city's first church, the beautiful little Holy Trinity, dwarfed now by highrises but still bravely standing. Down the road a little from the church, the Lion Arts Centre houses the work of avant-garde craft workers, glassblowers and potters and jewellers, an intricate display behind a glass wall that glimmers at dusk. After midnight, around the corner of North and West Terraces where a weathered marker tells you Colonel Light stood in the first days of 1837 to begin his survey of the city, you will sometimes see a wild-eyed homeless person or a young one reckless from drink or drugs emerge violently from the West Parklands as though spat out of the darkness and into the path of the oncoming traffic. Lives have been lost.

Back on North Terrace, much further east and far less full of life – for somehow you never see anyone entering or departing – is the Adelaide Club. This is a beautiful building of pleasing, modest dimensions, made of local stone relieved with red brick. The Australian flag flying from the balcony looks new, and is so big that it spoils the proportions of the building; the green shutters and window frames, however, are looking pretty shabby these days for 'the city's most exclusive gentlemen's club'. Formed in 1863, the Adelaide Club used to have a reputation for being the true seat of power in South Australia, but this is regarded by most, though perhaps not by the members, as a wild exaggeration. According to their website, ladies may attend private functions (if dressed appropriately), but under 'How many members do we have?' it says 'Gentlemen: 974. Ladies: N/A.'

Across from the Adelaide Club, on the shady side of the terrace outside the wall of Government House, there's a motley but somehow pleasing assortment of statues in granite, bronze or marble, including the fearless Boer War soldier on his noble horse, a delicate and mostly naked Venus, King Edward VII with assorted allegorical females deployed under his feet, that sweet-faced ladies' man Robert Burns looking deceptively girlie till you get to the stone bulge in his tight breeches, Matthew Flinders with his sword and sextant looming black and huge over everybody's head, and Australia's first-ever female judge, later Governor of South Australia, Dame Roma Mitchell, deep in thought yet somehow still demure in a low antique-looking armchair. A long way further east along North Terrace, Aboriginal people who have travelled down from their communities in the state's far north to get medical treatment sit on the forecourt of the Royal Adelaide Hospital, looking dazed. It's a fair bet that neither they nor the swooping boys from the skate park nor the satin girls from the nightclubs nor the homeless people from the Parklands are ever likely to see the inside of the Adelaide Club.

Since the tramline was extended north from Victoria Square along King William Street, around the corner into North Terrace, westwards past the University of South Australia and all the way out through the Parklands to the Entertainment Centre in the inner northwestern suburb of Hindmarsh, it has changed the flow of energy around the Adelaide streets. Simply in terms of noise and movement, a stranger would now probably pinpoint the intersection of North Terrace and King William Street as the real heart of the city. Almost everyone moving through that intersection is headed for somewhere else, but that is how the heart works, pumping blood around the body.

One street south, there's the closest thing

Adelaide has to a King's Cross: Hindley Street (it rhymes, however inappropriately, with kindly, not spindly), where bars and pubs with pokies abound, where the sex shops and the strip joints cluster, where people in assorted states of consciousness shout and fight, where the street life is noisy and incomprehensible, where everything seems old and nothing ever seems completely clean, and where, as the night wears on, people start yelling out from cars, pissing in alleyways, puking in corners and, occasionally, bleeding from the head. Hindley Street has its own police station, and it is always busy. But in the middle of all this, you'll find the headquarters of the excellent Adelaide Symphony Orchestra, the offices of the state's Department for the Arts, an entire university campus, and Imprints, the best bookshop in the city.

Hindley Street was the first port of call for settlers and sailors alike, for all who had come ashore at Port Adelaide and travelled from there via Port Road to the centre of the city. From its earliest days, Hindley Street provided the things that many of these people were after: wine, women and song, or perhaps I mean sex, drugs and music-hall. Adelaideans and visitors alike were to go on mocking and complaining about the perceived absence of these things for the next century and a half – 'Find me a bar, or a girl or guitar,' sings Paul Kelly in 'Adelaide' – but the truth was (and still is) that you could find anything you wanted in Adelaide if you knew where to look. The young Scottish actress and exhibitionist Thistle Anderson, viciously trashing the respectable citizens in 1905 in her little book *Arcadian Adelaide*, informs us that this city of self-proclaimed respectability and virtue contained eight opium dens (where Melbourne, at three times its size, had only seven) – not to mention the swarms of teenage prostitutes, some of them trained by their mothers. She seems to have known what she was talking about, too, though she doesn't say how she came by the knowledge.

Hindley Street was originally the city's commercial centre, though that focus shifted later in the 19th century and 'the shops' are currently to be found mainly on Rundle Street, half of which was turned into a pedestrian mall in the days of Premier Don Dunstan, and under his unrelenting pressure. The department stores and specialty chainstores are concentrated here, and Rundle Mall is busy and colourful enough in the daytime, but it turns sinister and deserted at night after all the shops have closed: the little booths along the middle of the mall have their unbeautiful shutters down, and the strip is dimly lit and empty but for the occasional homeless person huddled in a doorway or the odd small knot of aimless, faceless boys in hoodies, looking for action or trouble. Further east where the mall becomes a street again, in the section generally referred to as 'the East End', there are suddenly more people and more lights; what used to be a shabby part of town in the 1960s and 1970s was extensively developed in the 1980s and is now full of restaurants, cafes, cinemas, shops, pubs and bars.

Only the ghosts of specialty shops that were here before the transformation remain, and two of the most memorable of these were run by colourful and adventurous Adelaide businesswomen. No physical trace remains of Sophie van Rood's vintage clothes business, The Banana Room, which was located there in the 1970s, before 'vintage' went mainstream and the business relocated to North Adelaide. Then you could still get beautiful clothes from the 1920s and earlier that were made of silk and lace and *crêpe de chine* yet still affordable on a student budget, if you were prepared to live on brown rice for a few weeks. Salvaged from deceased-estate auctions, op shops, rubbish dumps and garage sales, van Rood's collection of 19th and early 20th century clothing was of such quality that 13 items from it are now displayed in Sydney's Powerhouse Museum, including a velvet cloche hat from the 1920s and an Indian muslin dress from circa 1810.

Nearby, there was one of Adelaide's best-known and most successful businesses: the small but packed emporium of the legendary Miss Gladys Sym Choon, who sold napery, china, lingerie, embroidery and lace, and belonged to a business family that had a monopoly throughout the state on the sale of fireworks. She opened her own shop, The China Gift Store, in 1923, when she was 18. She travelled annually to China on combined business and family trips, and was the first woman in South Australia to import goods for sale, and the first to form a business in her own right. Her premises now house a business that has preserved her shop-front façade and still uses her name. Like Sophie van Rood's, her shop in that down-at-heel stretch of Rundle Street in the 1970s was like a ruby in the dust, each store housing a collection of things from other times or places that smelled of spice or fragrant wood or the ghosts of perfumes that had long since ceased to be made.

But one of the city's most dramatic transformations over the last few decades has taken place in a different part of town. As a schoolgirl in neighbouring Grote Street, I saw the Gouger Street of the late 1960s as a quiet, drab strip whose many vacant frontages featured those sad signs of failure, the piles of unopened mail slid under the door to mingle with dust and dead blowflies, and whose only spots of interest were the exotic, mysterious and – to Adelaideans – somehow shady shops selling Turkish and Persian carpets and rugs. It was not a prosperous part of town; one street north on Grote Street, across the road from Adelaide Girls' High, where she was employed to teach art, the Adelaide painter Barbara Robertson was painting the poor and disadvantaged whose meagre, dusty back yards her studio overlooked.

But energy and money can flow around a city in unexpected ways; Gouger Street has been enlivened over the last few decades by various developments and projects. The building of the Hilton Hotel, the continued flourishing of the Adelaide Central Market, the growth of Adelaide's little Chinatown on the western side of the market and its very little Little India down Market Street on the other side of the road, and most recently the new tramline, have all either contributed to or resulted from the fact that Gouger Street has been transformed from the shabby little street of the 1960s into another long and lively strip of restaurants, cafes, clubs and bars. On Saturday mornings there are so many shoppers at the Central Market that your chances of not running into at least one person you know (for this is Adelaide) are very small, and the Gouger Street cafes overflow with tired caffeine-seekers pulling shopping carts or pushing prams and strollers in which small children are half-buried under the shopping: weekend papers, baguettes, tomato seedlings, Portuguese custard tarts with cinnamon, unsalted butter from France, huge free-range eggs from Kangaroo Island and the foliage of bok choy and spinach and lilies. On hot nights the crowds spill out into the roadway from the restaurant strips where Thailand cosies up to Argentina, Italy to Vietnam and Sichuan Province to Spain, while in the Mars Bar, which advertises itself as 'Adelaide's only gay and lesbian night club', the clever young drag queens parody a bygone model of femininity and – perhaps in homage to Adelaide's best-known former madam and would-be politician, Stormy Summers – give themselves sibilant, witty, urban-sounding names: Victoria Square, Summer Clearance, Selma Derriere.

And while Gouger Street is neither seedy nor complex in the way that Hindley Street is both, all the same, late at night, there are places there that a cautious person might think twice about entering, and occasionally some violent private feud erupts into its public space. 'The fabric has changed on Gouger Street,' said Adelaide City Councillor Francis Wong a few years ago in a triumph of delicate euphemism, after two shoot-outs, at least one of which involved bikers, resulted in the installation of security cameras along the street. Yet there is still a strange but widespread conviction in the public mind, even after decades of serial killings and other bizarre murders, that such things just don't happen in little old Adelaide. Gouger Street is another source of pronunciation uncertainty, but in this case there seems to be no consensus even among Adelaide citizens; opinion is fairly evenly divided between 'GOOD-jer' and 'GOO-jer', so visitors should feel free to choose. Given that the man for whom the street was named – the first Colonial Secretary, Robert Gouger – was of Huguenot descent, the 'correct' pronunciation is probably 'Goo-ZHAY', which nobody would dream of saying except in jest.

Gouger Street runs into Victoria Square, which

the map suggests should be the most promising and important site in town, but has in fact been the most consistently disappointing and vexatious: the large green park in the geometric centre of the city, hedged about by traffic arrangements and encroaching roads and footpaths and tramlines and tracks where development has inevitably nibbled away at it, has long been the locus of disgruntlement and worse among Adelaide's citizens, city councillors and traders.

The trouble with Victoria Square is inherent in the Adelaide plan, for such a design, like a squared-off mandala, leads the feet, the eye and the mind inexorably to the centre, and sets up a ferment of unconscious expectations that some goal or climax or treasure will be found there. Even a minotaur would be better than nothing. But this steadily shrinking piece of broken-up lawn, with its assortment of 19th century statues, its horrible petunia-heavy municipal flowerbeds and its labyrinthine, counter-intuitive arrangements for pedestrians to get from one side to another, has nothing in it of a weight to match the aesthetic, social or spiritual expectations of a centre that the city's layout inevitably sets up. Historian Peter Morton shows that the problem was clear as early as 1878:

The council debated this year whether to drive King William Street through the centre of the square to make a grander thoroughfare, but … the motion was withdrawn. For the present, Victoria Square continued to be two poorly-fenced and rather scruffy rectangles of lawns and trees at the geometrical centre of the city. It was only the emblematic heart, however, because the commercial life of the city had already concentrated itself in the streets further north. At various times there had been proposals to situate the parliament, the university and the cathedral in the square, but they had come to nothing.

Any one of those three things – a political, an intellectual or a spiritual centre – would have given Victoria Square enough symbolic heft and significance to make it congruent with its central position and to make people feel that they have actually arrived somewhere. Morton's word 'emblematic' here is misleading; the whole problem with Victoria Square was, and remains, precisely that it isn't emblematic of anything. But there is one exception: its most potent and inspiring feature is the pair of tall flagpoles flying huge Australian and Aboriginal flags side by side. This is the first place in the world where, in 1972, the newly designed Aboriginal flag was raised. The square has dual signage; like other sites around the city, it has been officially accorded its Aboriginal name, Tarndanyangga, the Place of the Red Kangaroo, a significant site for the Kaurna people.

But however important these symbols and gestures may be, and they're a great deal better than nothing, there's not a lot of point in putting up dual signage and flying the Aboriginal flag when the 'dry zone' ruling introduced by the Adelaide City Council in 2001, prohibiting drinking in public areas of the city, drove the Aboriginal people out of what used to be one of their favourite, and important, meeting places. It might as well be called Empty Gesture Square. The council meeting went along lines that were predictable for anyone who knew the players and had been following the story:

> On April 2, Adelaide City Council voted to make the streets and parks of the inner CBD a 'dry zone'.
>
> … David Wright, chairperson of the Inner City Agencies Group, addressed the council and pointed out that the dry zone targeted Aboriginal people who traditionally gather in open spaces and are most often refused service in pubs …

Former QC Elliott Johnson also spoke eloquently against the dry zone. He said a dry zone results in more indigenous people in prison, in breach of the recommendations of the Royal Commission into Black Deaths in Custody.

The motion to support the dry zone was put by Councillor Michael Harbison, a Liberal candidate for the state seat of Adelaide. His claim that he could not walk through Victoria Square without falling over drunken Aborigines was greeted with derision from [the] public gallery …

Councillor Greg Mackie, speaking against the motion, told the council that there were already laws in place to deal with drunken behaviour. He added that people who were likely to break the dry zone laws were also unlikely to be able to pay the fines and would be incarcerated.

Two days later in the *City Messenger*, political commentator Terry Plane wrote that:

the dry zone proposal did not arise in response to the problems of public drunkenness around such city hotels as the Havelock and Seven Stars [two of Adelaide's upmarket watering holes]. Young, respectable, middle-class drunks … regularly cause a mess and nuisance in Hutt and Carrington streets. Is this dry zone aimed at them?

Eight years later there were renewed calls to abolish the dry zone ruling. Sister Janet Mead of 'singing nun' fame, who was named South Australian of the Year for 2005 in recognition of her commitment to social justice, is the founder of the Adelaide Day Care Centre for Homeless Persons and is well placed to understand the effects of the ruling:

> Since the dry zone has been in, Aborigines have been pushed out of Victoria Square, their traditional meeting place, and the city. Several have met death and injury crossing West Terrace. In effect, it has discriminated against Aborigines and resulted in them being moved on or put in jail while whites are drinking outside pubs and clubs and in alfresco restaurants or office parties in the squares.

The artist Juan Davila, making the same point in an essay on Adelaide, also regarded the perversity of the ban from a different angle: 'The declaration of dry zones – no drinking alcohol in the public spaces – as an affirmation of a will for order can be read as a perversion, given the dependence of the economy on the wine industry.' That conflict is likely to be ongoing, with strong feelings and predictable arguments on both sides.

Long pre-dating the matter of the dry zone, Victoria Square is — and seems always to have been — constructed by Adelaideans as a serious problem about which something must be done, often to the perplexity of international visitors who can't see anything wrong with it. Plans are perpetually being made and then scrapped, though the new tramline went ahead and in some ways has transformed the square, with many more people now moving through it. Adelaide columnist and broadcaster Peter Goers devoted a whole *Sunday Mail* column in 2007 to a list of suggestions about what we could do with Victoria Square, notable among which were 'A big nursing home — a fitting symbol for Adelaide' and 'Here's a novel idea — a beautiful park full of trees with the traffic going around it'. Or, he says, 'Let's just put up a big sign: "Welcome to the centre of Adelaide, where nothing ever happens."'

On the reverse side of this city map there is another of smaller scale but larger scope, showing the inner and outer suburbs. Now the extended map suggests bigger, more complicated things. Kaurna elder Uncle Lewis Yerloburka O'Brien writes about the city of Adelaide as the site of the Red Kangaroo Dreaming, discussing the importance of Kaurna sites underlying the streets and musing about the effects of burial grounds. O'Brien draws a map on which is outlined, following the lines of the city streets, the silhouette of a stylised kangaroo whose tail is the city end of Port Road. Its spine is North Terrace, and it could flick the Wine Centre off the back of its ear. This is a fanciful product of O'Brien's stated desire to see the peaceful coexistence of Kaurna culture with the contemporary city, and looking at the diagram it seems like just too much of a stretch – that is one Picasso-esque kangaroo – but Port Road is my route into the city from home, and since I read O'Brien's book I can't drive it any more without thinking of myself zooming down the slope of the roo-tail like a child on a slippery-dip. For better or worse, the streets in question, as I walk or drive along them now, are the lines of the cubist kangaroo: the tail, the chest, the paw.

If you pan out further you can see other things again. Because the design of the city is so symmetrical and converges so strongly on a single centre, the map, when it includes outer suburbs, looks disconcertingly like a spiderweb: not the mad messy kind, but the beautiful orb-weaver's wheel, with the anchoring spokes of arterial roads radiating out of the city and the cross-streets strung between them, and the statue of Queen Victoria, the black-clad widow, immobile at the heart of the design.

On this reverse-side map, you can see that greater Adelaide exists in a state of ongoing urban sprawl to the north and south. Built on a fertile strip of coastal plain between the Adelaide Hills and the coastline of St Vincent's Gulf, the city can spread in only two directions, prevented from expanding east and west by the Adelaide Hills, part of the Mount Lofty Ranges, on one side and the sea on the other. If you head east, the Hills rise abruptly: one minute you are driving sedately along a busy arterial road and the next you are thundering up the freeway at 100 km/h, with bushland on either side of you and a steep rise ahead beyond the Heysen Tunnel, which, with the new section of freeway that encompasses it, is the city's single biggest development of recent years. The tunnel has made the trip through the Hills shorter and less hazardous but has eliminated some of its spectacular views and some of its romance, though it's still possible that having driven into the tunnel on your way out of town on a clear day or night even in summer, you will emerge from it into thick fog. This is the micro-climate of the pretty Hills town of Crafers, Adelaide's answer to the mythical Scottish village of Brigadoon, for like that eerie spot it periodically disappears into the mist. It's as though the negotiation of the Crafers fog is a test you must pass in order to get into Adelaide, or out of it.

Viewed from the coast or from the plain, the Adelaide Hills are pillowy, low and purple. Their highest peak, the optimistically named Mount Lofty, dominates the horizon, catches the eye, and provides immediate orientation. It doesn't look at all lofty from here, but when you're up there at the summit in the dark, looking down at the pattern of the city lights spread out like a sequined black cloth on the table-flat plain between the Hills and the sea, it feels higher than we know it to be. To the north, the Mount Lofty Ranges stretch beyond the boundaries of the city to the Barossa Valley and onwards; to the south they curve protectively westward around the southern side of the city to meet the coast, their hills and valleys stretching gently out into the waters of the gulf like the paws of a giant golden sphinx.

While visual artists have usually tended to paint the Hills from the perspective of the plain, the best verbal descriptions we have are from writers describing what it's like to be up in them. For Adelaide novelist Peter Goldsworthy it's nothing short of heaven:

> The day has taken its name to heart, a Sunday
> from the glory box of Sundays, a luminous
> morning saturated with sunlight and parrots …
> the world outside the car, wholly blue and gold,
> seems almost too much … Each valley is a little
> deeper and greener than the last, and each ridge, a
> little higher and bluer, seems another step in some
> sort of ascension.

Mark Twain was travelling in the other direction, down towards the city: visiting the Antipodes in 1895, he had caught the train from Melbourne but left it in the Hills to travel down to the city in a horse-drawn carriage: 'colour, colour, colour everywhere … the skies blue, and not a shred of cloud to mar the downpour of brilliant sunshine … the immense plain lay spread out below and stretching away into dim distances'. The Australian writer Hal Porter, also travelling from Melbourne by train on his way to a teaching job in Adelaide during World War II, woke up not long after dawn in his sleeping compartment and looked out of the window, whereupon his habitual undertone of mockery and self-mockery seems, like Twain's, to have deserted him and been replaced with awe:

> There are hills. Immeasurably ancient, abraded low and smooth, they seem young, boneless, pagan, sprawling ... The hills are not stitched to the sky. There is no seam of horizon. The sky is seen to curve up from far far behind the hills as if the hills, the earth, are centrally contained in a globe of glass hanging plumb and steady from the rafters of infinity.

But the Hills do not have a monopoly on blue and gold. To me this combination is the essence of South Australia: brazen suns in hot skies of virginal blue, beachside layering of colour from creamy pale-gold sand through sea to sky in two or more different blues, and in the hinterlands of city and coast the endless fields of wheat and barley, the light and the landscape a mashup of 'The Song of Australia' with 'On First Looking Into Chapman's Homer': *Much have I travelled in the realms of gold, and all above is azure bright.*

You can even see it in the heart of town. On

some days, in some lights, the Adelaide CBD is much like that of any other modern city: a forest of upended boxes in subtly discordant colours. A boxy, sheep-coloured edifice butts up to a gunmetal-grey office tower; a pale caramel hotel towers over something in steel, glass and black granite; a highrise apartment block, trimmed in a shade of synthetic turquoise, heaves itself up inappropriately into the true blue of the sky. But at other times, if you go up onto a city balcony or rooftop — a third dimension that no map of the city will show you — in the late afternoon of a warm day, something in the haze and the softness of the air transforms the colours and the geometry of Adelaide into those of Tuscany. Straight lines and angles fade into the background, nudging curves and arches to the fore; garlands and gargoyles of plaster and stone leap into high relief. And the clashing pastels resolve themselves into gentle, harmonious, pre-dusk variations on the theme of blue and gold: ice-blue and russet, violet and terracotta, powder-blue and buttermilk, lavender and silver-gilt, lilac and amber.

People reading about these Adelaide streets will immediately recall their own experience of them, if they have any. The simple, pretty grid pattern is one thing, but an experiential or cognitive map is quite another, a palimpsest or layering of sense-memory, mood-memory, and the vivid recollection of images, emotions and events. For locals, in addition, there's the impossibly complex set of associations and projections that attach to a home town's central role in the process of self-fashioning. When I look at the map, I see the words 'Waymouth Street' and there rises before me the image of a 15-year-old Greek boy on crutches trying to eat a hamburger in the rain in 1967. 'Wakefield Street' means the rich soprano voice and festive, tent-like purple dress of the woman who sang 'Once in Royal David's City' at Midnight Mass – the first I'd ever attended, and strictly as a guest – in St Francis Xavier Cathedral on Christmas Eve in 1975. 'Sir Edwin Smith Avenue' recalls the scent of the sun-warmed rose garden in the grounds of the hospital where my mother died on a summer's morning in 1999, and where one of my oldest and dearest friends was born, also on a summer's morning, in 1952; 'Archer Street' conjures up a dark man in his mid-50s walking up the street in the hot sun to meet me for a drink, 20 years after the first drink we ever met for, the splintering sunlight so blinding that I can't see his face, only his walk and silhouette, but that is enough. What rises first to full consciousness in this particular map-based form of word association is like opera: it's usually about love and death.

And so when I talk to friends who grew up here about the map of Adelaide, I find it oddly difficult to get them to think of it purely as a patterned object; they immediately begin to invest it with emotion and history, and to talk about that instead. Only one, the most concrete thinker among them, sees immediately what I mean when I compare the map to a Moorish tile, and is interested by that; the others slide immediately from the image of a piece of paper with a pattern on it into reflections on their own long and complicated relationships with the city. One starts talking wistfully about the squares of London, which is where, in our youth, she always wanted to be instead of here. Another says he thinks that any map of Adelaide should be of the medieval or pirate-map kind, with little drawings of serpents, and ships with sails, and treasure-chests, and warnings: *Here be dragons.*

3
The Painting

Twenty years is a long time to spend working on a painting, and perhaps it was more. Like several other things about 'The Proclamation of South Australia 1836', begun in 1856, the date of completion is unclear. The artist and engraver Charles Hill was earnest in his desire to paint, as a matter of historical record, the truth of an event that took place almost a decade before it could have been photographed, and two decades before he started work on it. Many of the figures in the painting are individual portraits of real, identifiable people, and commentary on it over the years has suggested it was very important to him that the painting should stand as a truthful historical record of the occasion.

Yet there are anomalies in it, historical and other. There are mysteries.

The painting is dated 'c. 1856–76' by the Art Gallery of South Australia, which bought it in

1936. There is a copy of it, to scale at 133.3 x 274.3cm, on permanent display at the Bay Discovery Centre in Moseley Square, Glenelg. Even knowing its dimensions, you don't realise how enormous it is until you are standing in front of it, trying at once to be close enough to see all the detail and far enough away to take it in whole. A long, large rectangle in landscape orientation, painted in oils on a canvas bigger than a single bed, it shows a gathering of over 150 people, and is painted in fine detail, with a broad, deep swathe of landscape in the background. It depicts the moment that the Colony of South Australia was officially proclaimed, as imagined by the artist. Hill also provided a key: a drawing with all of the painting's figures and features sketched in outline and numbered, so you can work out who everybody is.

Colonel William Light had been appointed Surveyor-General to the colony and charged with deciding on a site for the city and surveying its 'town acres' for purchase by colonists. But he had been delayed for so long and by so many different things, some of them ridiculous, that the site of Adelaide had still not been decided by the time the first appointed Governor of South Australia, Captain John Hindmarsh of His Majesty's

Navy, arrived from Portsmouth on the *Buffalo* and anchored in Holdfast Bay, where a temporary village of tents and huts had been set up a mile or so back from the beach by officials and colonists who had arrived earlier in the year. But technically speaking the colony had come into being months before the Governor or any other official arrived in it, on 19 February 1836, the day the British Government issued the Letters Patent creating it as a political entity and defining its boundaries. Still, the presence of the Governor at this temporary colonial camp meant that South Australia was now in practice as well as in theory a province of Great Britain, and the day the Governor arrived it was ceremonially proclaimed.

The Colonial Secretary, Robert Gouger, had arrived almost two months earlier on the *Africaine* with a boatload of colonists, his pregnant wife and his precious Cashmere goats. He was by now well set up, with a floored double tent, a reed hut, an enclosure for his goats and chickens and a meticulous habit of writing regularly in his journal, where on the evening of 28 December 1836, he described the ceremony that Charles Hill, 20 years later, would paint. Getting up on that hot morning, Gouger went outside to let the goats out and saw the Governor's ship sailing up the gulf:

> At 3 o'clock the marines from the *Buffalo* were
> drawn up in a line, and the whole of the colonists
> assembled in front of my tent … I administered
> to the governor the oaths of office. We then held
> a Council in my tent for the purpose of agreeing
> upon a proclamation requiring all to obey the laws
> … The Commission was then read in public …
> and the festivities were kept up to a late hour.

At this point Adelaide itself, as yet, existed as not much more than an idea: the city had a name and a handful of increasingly impatient would-be inhabitants living in tents and reed huts, with no houses and no streets to put them on. Indeed, it did not yet even have — at least not officially — a site, only this calm bay in the quiet waters of St Vincent's Gulf. Although the Surveyor-General and his team were close to a decision about the city site, debate among some of the people in the painting continued to rage about the suitability of other possible locations for the capital. But the hypothetical city had at least been named in advance: for the gentle Queen Adelaide, consort to King William IV.

It had been some years since the idea of a

Colony of South Australia was first mooted back in London. Historian Douglas Pike dates the earliest beginnings of the colony at 1829, when Edward Gibbon Wakefield met Robert Gouger. Wakefield, jailed for the abduction of a teenage heiress, had become interested in how his fellow prisoners had ended up there, and was developing schemes for successful emigration to the British colonies, including what he called 'systematic colonisation':

> Wakefield claimed that Australian colonies were suffering from chaotic granting of free land, shortage of labour and consequent dependence on convicts. He argued that if settlement were concentrated, waste lands of the crown could be readily sold and the proceeds applied to the emigration of labourers, preferably young married couples … Sufficiency of labour and a congenial society would attract capital, encourage emigration, assure prosperity, and justify the rights of a colony to elect representatives to its own legislature.

Gouger was already interested in colonisation, but it was Wakefield's scheme that made him focus on Australia and then on South Australia, in the region where the explorer Charles Sturt had said a likely site would be found. And it was Gouger who worked hard over the next six years on making the South Australian colony a reality. One of the ironies of the establishment of Adelaide and of the way the city saw itself for many years — free of the convict stain and therefore superior — is that the earliest plans for the colony were made by two men who had both seen the inside of a jail: Gouger spent some time in prison for debt to a printer, incurred while promoting the cause of a South Australian colony, while Wakefield had abducted and then eloped with a 15-year-old heiress — something he had already done once before. He had not only got away with it the first time, but had inherited that young woman's considerable fortune after she died of child-bed fever. Perhaps it's just as well he never actually set foot in South Australia.

But even without knowing all this history, without the artist's key, without the painting's title, there are still many things that a viewer could deduce about what's happening. It's a group of figures in a landscape, but it's also clearly a historical painting, in which some real-life ceremony of importance is taking place before an assorted crowd: men and women, military and civilian, black and white, adults and children, people and dogs.

They are sitting, standing or lounging in what they would probably have called 'out of doors', wearing clothing typical of England towards the middle of the 19th century.

The colours are not English, though, and neither are the trees or the light. The trees are of olive-drab shade and untidy shape, the soil in the foreground a sandy colour with a few clumps here and there of spearlike grass. The sky is a bleached blue, shading at its brightest point almost to white. The light is clear and unforgiving. In the background there are a few tents, and a gum tree whose trunk is bent right over into an arch that almost touches the ground, with new branches springing upwards from its curved-over main trunk, and a handful of adolescent boys who have adventurously climbed up to the highest point of the arch. On the horizon there rises a range of modest hills, of a dark and smoky purple–blue.

In the centre of the picture, the focus of the crowd's attention as well as of the viewer's, stands a small group of men who clearly have official status, as evidenced by their clothes: the blacks, reds, whites and blues of military, clerical or formal civilian dress, with here and there some splashes of gold against the navy's blue. One man is in the full regalia of a senior naval officer, another is recognisable as a cleric and scholar by his collar, cap and gown. A third man is dressed in day clothes, standing a little apart with his back to the viewer but unmistakably a part of this central group; a fourth, central to the composition, is a dark-haired man in the red and white of the British Army, who has about him a familiar look. And the fifth, elegantly dressed in civilian black, is holding a document that seems to be at the heart of the story this picture is telling. If you quarter the painting, you can see that this document is at its very centre, where the vertical axis meets the horizontal; the vertical axis goes through the highest mountain peak and straight down the middle of the figure in the red coat before it arrives at the document, on which you can see, if you look closely, the words 'South Australia' and '1836'.

Around and behind this ceremonial group of important men, sailors and marines form two parallel lines along one side of the crowd, and a single row of soldiers is ranged along the back of it, all standing to attention. There are at least two dozen ladies in bonnets and shawls; a few of the lucky ones are sitting on fallen logs or stumps, but most are standing. People on the edges of the crowd seem by their dress and demeanour to be representing the humbler classes. There are assorted children, a couple of excited dogs, and, in the distance, a number of Aboriginal figures who watch curiously as the ceremony proceeds. A few steps to the right of the central group and towards the foreground, two men are labouring at the foot of a bare flagpole to raise a flag still half-unfolded on the ground but recognisable as the Union Jack.

Those involved in the ceremony seem stiff and formal, especially the thick-set, grey-haired man in the most splendid of the uniforms, but on the fringes of the crowd there are little bursts of liveliness. To the left, behind the soldiers and marines, a young mother is holding out her hands to retrieve a delighted-looking baby from the arms of its father. Over on the right, three children and a little white dog are engrossed in some sort of game. Near the flagpole, another, larger dog, a black one this time, is excitedly jumping up on his young master, while the older boys climbing the bent gum tree in the background are clearly not paying any attention to the ceremony. To the right, quite a few people in the crowd are being distracted from the proceedings by something happening in the other direction, beyond the picture's frame. Most of the other people in the painting, those paying attention to the ceremony, look serious; some look sombre and one or two look downright miserable. The handful of Aboriginal people in the background seem both more comfortable and more interested in the ceremony than many of the colonists in the crowd.

There's a real tenderness for human nature in all this: a realisation that a long voyage might be an exhausting experience; that a temperature recorded as 103° Fahrenheit – 39° Celsius – in the afternoon sun might render the heavy 19th-century clothing unbearable; that attention can be easily distracted; and that even the most momentous occasion means little to children, and to animals nothing at all. There's some implicit gentle mockery of the important men and their important paper in the detail to the left (the besotted young parents playing with their baby), and to the right (the excited dogs playing with the children). There's a hint of how hot it is in the flagging of the crowd's attention, the visible discomfort on some of their faces, and the relative physical ease of the children in loose light clothes and the Aboriginal people in no clothes at all. And there's a recognition that here, already, was the beginning of a society, in a city that didn't yet exist.

Three days from the event depicted so fully and carefully in the painting, the Surveyor-General will confirm his choice of a site – a few miles northeast of Holdfast Bay – and the detailed business of surveying, of marking out the streets and squares and parklands and 'town acres', will begin. In the meantime, the document being read out is the Proclamation of the Colony of South Australia. The man in black is the Governor's secretary, George Stevenson, and although the point of this gathering is to proclaim the existence of the colony to the settlers (though presumably the settlers knew about it already, for here they are), Stevenson appears to be directly addressing his boss – the stocky grey-haired man in the most resplendent uniform: Governor John Hindmarsh, naval officer and vice-regal representative of King William IV.

It seems odd to be looking at a painting about a document without being able to see what the document says. The Proclamation is read every year in a ceremony at the location where this first gathering is said to have taken place; given the flowery style and labyrinthine sentences of the period, especially on such formal and portentous occasions as this, the document seems short and abrupt, even stark. 'In announcing to the Colonists of His Majesty's

Province of South Australia, the establishment of the Government,' it says, in part:

> I hereby call upon them to conduct themselves
> on all occasions with order and quietness, duly to
> respect the laws, and by a course of industry and
> sobriety, by the practice of sound morality, and a
> strict observance of the Ordinances of Religion,
> to prove themselves worthy to be the founders of
> a great and free Colony.

The fact that most of the rest of this document is taken up with promises, injunctions and even veiled threats about the fair and decent treatment of the Aboriginal people suggests that the South Australian officials had already heard the tales of poisonings and massacres coming out of the colonies along the eastern seaboard, or even from colonised countries further abroad, and were determined that South Australia should generate no such tales. Robert Gouger confirms this in his book *South Australia in 1837, in a Series of Letters.* He wrote:

> Though I landed in South Australia without
> any feeling of fear of the natives, I nevertheless
> felt great anxiety respecting them. I knew full
> well that if the first rencontre with them should
> be unfriendly, that the effect might be truly

deplorable. So many miseries have been sustained
by these unoffending creatures in different parts
of the continent, and so unrelenting has been
the persecution of them, even though the first
cause of quarrel has generally been an aggression
of the whites, that I felt particularly anxious
one instance, at least, of kind treatment, should
be known in history – that the annals of our
province should be unstained by native blood.

It's as strong an indication as any of the idealism
and optimism that dominated the founding of the
colony. The first paragraph of the Proclamation is
equally interesting in its idealistic foreshadowing
of a future: those who regard Adelaide even to
this day as complacent, boring and smug will not
be surprised by such words as 'order', 'quietness',
'respect', 'industry', 'sobriety' and 'morality'. The
Adelaide colonists began as they meant to go on.

On paper, anyway. After the official ceremony
was completed, the Governor's party retired in an
orderly fashion back to the ship on which they had
arrived that morning. But back on shore, the sailors
got drunk, the Aborigines set fire to the trees, and
most of the colonists stayed up all night partying
on the beach, for it was far too hot to sleep. The
people in this painting will learn over the coming

years that this is no more than they should expect of Adelaide in summer: still blue heat with an unbearable glitter, heat enough to mummify you, and to remind you that you are just beyond the edge of the desert.

The last remnants of the Old Gum Tree, nothing of it left now but its bowed trunk and a couple of sad leafless branches, are held in place with cement and shaded by a roof-like structure in a quiet little park in Glenelg North. Plaques and interpretive signs abound; the site is part of the Holdfast Bay tourist trail. It's 28 December 2010, the 174th anniversary of the events depicted in this painting; along with hundreds of other citizens of Adelaide, I arrive at the site for the annual Proclamation Day ceremony, where speeches are made and the Proclamation is ritually read out once more.

As in Hill's painting, it's a warm blue day; the air is soft and still as the cool early morning is warmed up by the rising sun. Today is the Third Day of Christmas, as I am reminded by the assorted white things I can see drifting through the enamelled sky: three cirrus clouds, two pelicans and a slow-setting chubby half-moon. The crowd is a 2010 version of 1836; just as in Hill's painting, there are couples, family groups, little dogs, bored children, people trying to shade themselves from the sun, lines of uniformed figures, a knot of officialdom at the centre of the composition, and some watchful Aboriginal people standing quietly in the distance, across the street from the park.

The program says that both Premier Mike Rann and Prime Minister Julia Gillard are among the speakers. At this moment in their respective political fortunes, neither is especially popular, and I fear that one or both might be booed or heckled, but I have forgotten the capacity of Adelaideans to sit quietly and reasonably and listen to what people have to say.

Governor Kevin Scarce speaks before either of them. He is not only a big improvement both intellectually and politically on his earliest predecessor, the arrogant, quarrelsome and not very bright Governor Hindmarsh, but, as a Rear-Admiral, he outranks him as well. He speaks of the mixed reception afforded the asylum-seekers who in recent weeks arrived and were housed at an army facility at Inverbrackie in the Adelaide Hills, where some local residents had protested along predictable lines while larger numbers went out of their way to be welcoming and supportive. The Governor links these events to the arrival of the first white South Australians, and stresses the values of tolerance and freedom on which the state was officially built.

His speech is greeted warmly. The Prime Minister, who grew up here, begins by remarking on the good luck of Adelaideans to have perfect weather for this celebration, and reminds us how easy it is on such a day to forget about the people whose lives, as she speaks, are being caught up and spun out of control by the floods that have just begun in Queensland, where she is headed later today. She too speaks of the importance of citizens looking after each other. Between them, the Governor and the Prime Minister have effortlessly lifted a provincial celebration above the level of its immediate concerns and emphasised the connectedness of South Australia to the rest of the country and the rest of the world.

It is left for a Kaurna elder, a woman unnamed in the program but given, in the order of speakers, both the first and last word, to point out that some of the promises made in the Proclamation have not been kept, and that some of the conditions in the Letters Patent that had been issued legally establishing the province in February 1836, which made it mandatory to safeguard 'the rights of any Aboriginal Natives of the said Province to the actual occupation and enjoyment in their own persons or in the persons of their descendants of any Lands therein now actually occupied or enjoyed by such Natives' have not yet been met.

Given the prime last spot on the list of speakers, she speaks at length, repetitively, haranguingly. She is not a good speaker, and appears to be in failing health. She is disquieting on a number of fronts. She is out to embarrass the Premier, and does. The crowd sits quietly and listens to that too, for the 1836 wording is quite unambiguous, and everything she says is true.

Like its first day, the colony's first few years were a great deal more noisy, disorderly, disrespectful and drunk than the Proclamation recommends or than Hill's painting suggests, and that's just the men in high places: the pages of early South Australian history are littered with disagreements, dramas, quarrels, sulks, bruised egos, wars of attrition, and in one case a fist-fight in the street – between the usually affable Robert Gouger and the heavy-drinking and quarrelsome Colonial Treasurer, Osmond Gilles — that saw both men arrested and ended in Gouger being suspended from his position as Colonial Secretary and sent back to England.

Robert Gouger occupies a strange place in Hill's painting. He is near the middle and towards the foreground, yet he has his back to the viewer. He is clearly part of the group of officials at the centre of proceedings, yet seems to be merely observing rather than taking an active part. He is both dressed and positioned in such a way as to make his figure stand out, and the viewer's eye is drawn to him. He's one of the few figures in the painting whose back is almost fully turned, but as far as capturing and conveying personality is concerned, his may be one of the most successful portraits here. Gouger looks as lively as anything, despite the fact that he is standing still and his face is hidden; leaning slightly forward, he appears to be taking a keen interest in the ceremonial proceedings. Unlike some of the solemn men in uniform and some of the po-faced ladies in bonnets, he seems energetic and engaged.

But even at only 34, Gouger does not look here like the adventurous visionary we find in his journals and correspondence. The Surveyor-General, Colonel William Light, was dark, slender, mysterious-looking and multi-talented, straight out of the pages of Jane Austen. Gouger, by contrast, seems, from the only full-face portrait of him that I can find, and from this painting, to have been a man whose only place in an Austen novel might have been as a butt of jokes in which the heroines would have had their ruthless conversational way, but who, being a man with a good heart, might have been rewarded with the hand of one of the lesser ladies in the end. Only 16 years younger than Light, he seems nonetheless to belong to a different era, an early Victorian rather than a late Georgian; where Light was an Austen hero, Gouger appears by both temperament and appearance to belong to an early Dickens novel, perhaps *The Pickwick Papers*, which was being published in serial instalments in 1836 and which he might even have been reading, waiting impatiently for the next instalment to arrive on the next ship. You can see in the Hill painting that Gouger is a little portly and prematurely balding; the full-face portrait shows a chubby face that is plain in every aspect except the eyes, which are large and dark, and seem full of liveliness and intelligence.

In the Proclamation painting, strands of thinning, gingerish hair curl round his shining pate, revealed by a hat most ill-advisedly removed from his head and clutched in both hands behind his back, exposing his scalp to the ferocious sunlight. He is wearing cream-coloured trousers that suit the weather (but do nothing at all for his figure), and must have often been grievously grubbied in the course of tent life in the Adelaide summer heat.

The colony of South Australia is quite as much his baby as the one to which his wife is shortly to give birth. Contrary to the key that identifies her in the painting as a small wedge of bonnet just visible behind her husband's head, Harriet Gouger was not standing in the crowd at 3pm that day; she was in her husband's tent, which is shown in the background of the painting, and while her husband administered the oaths of office to Governor Hindmarsh inside the tent and then sat down with the other officials to decide on the wording of the Proclamation before going outside to read it to the assembled crowd, the consumptive Harriet struggled with the heat and the early stages of labour.

The liveliness and eagerness captured in the figure of Gouger is not surprising given how long he had waited for this moment, and given that in any case 'his temperament was perhaps a little warm'. For almost eight years he had been working tirelessly to plan the colony, to drum up support for its establishment, to revive collapsed plans and replace discarded ones, to lobby everyone from the Duke of Wellington downwards to ensure the passage of the Bill through the British Parliament and then, most recently, to work at the heart of the colony and its management for its survival from its earliest days. In his journal he describes his own feelings at the moment captured by Hill's painting:

> Rapidly as my heart beat on this occasion – an occasion to which, during the years I had devoted to the prosecution of the enterprise, I dared sometimes to anticipate and rejoice in – I was not suffered long to bestow even one thought upon it … The Commission had hardly left my tent yesterday when the doctor was called in attendance upon my wife, who this morning at 6 o'clock gave the new province a son!

Five months later, on 3 June 1836, the first edition of the first Adelaide newspaper, *The South Australian Gazette and Colonial Register*, carried the following announcements, the one directly below the other:

BIRTH.

On December 29th, 1836, at Glenelg, Mrs. Robert Gouger, of a son.

DEATHS.

On March 14th, at Glenelg, of consumption, Harriet, wife of the Honorable Robert Gouger, aged thirty-two years; and

On March 15th, their son, Henry Hindmarsh, aged eleven weeks and one day.

Later that year, Gouger got embroiled in the public brawl with the Colonial Treasurer that saw him arrested, suspended and sent home, via Hobart Town, to England. He was now not only doubly bereaved, but disgraced as well. He arrived in London, however, to the news that Governor Hindmarsh had been recalled and replaced by Colonel Gawler, and that he himself had been restored to his position by the Colonisation Commission after the intervention of a number of fellow colonists on his behalf. June 1839 saw him back in Adelaide with his second wife, an English cousin; he was restored to his position and then, under Governor Grey, appointed Colonial Treasurer himself.

But the colony had fallen on desperate economic times and this affected Gouger not only in his new role as Treasurer but also in terms of his personal finances. What happened to him then can only be imagined, as I can find no specific description either of his behaviour or of his general state; one account refers to 'a mental affliction' and another says 'his mind gradually gave way'.

History has treated Gouger erratically. On reading various sources and putting them together, it seems clear that in terms of sheer effort and activity over time, he did more than any other single person, including Wakefield and Light, to establish the idea of a colony in South Australia, to set it up in a systematic way, to establish a polity and to keep its machinery going during the first few hard and chaotic years of settlement. His capacity for perseverance and sustained hard slog makes him seem a Martha to Wakefield's Mary, though really he was more like Light: both had visionary qualities, but were also happy to get their hands dirty with the housework of creating a city. In *Paradise of Dissent*, a book that over 50 years after its publication is still regarded as the definitive history of South Australia's early years, Douglas Pike expresses a high opinion of Gouger, as a man of principle, energy and integrity, and offers him a wistful eulogy:

The strain of office, together with the perplexities
of debt, brought on a mental malady which led to
his resignation in 1844. He died in London two
years later, too early to see the fulfillment of his
dreams for South Australia. In its toponymy he is
remembered today by no more than a city street
and an electorate. A range of mountains named
after him by an exploring governor turned out to
be a cloud formation. His courage and resolution
deserved better memorials.

There is still no memorial to Gouger that I can dis-
cover anywhere in Adelaide. The one full-face portrait of him that exists is almost never reproduced
in the histories or in other books about the city,
though portraits of Light, Hindmarsh and other,
lesser Adelaide luminaries abound. That one portrait is taken from a miniature, which seems poignant in the same way as the mountains that turned
out to be a cloud formation. The impression given
by accounts of his life is that he never stood still
for long enough to have his portrait painted; in the
miniature, he appears to be fidgeting.

An early historian of South Australia, the Rev-
erend John Blacket, observes that 'No monument
has been erected to his memory in South Australia,
but let the descendants of the early emigrants as

they read or speak of "Gouger-street," or walk through it, remember the deep debt of gratitude they owe to the man whose name it bears.' I don't know that many of us do. But Pike and Blacket and Gouger himself might all be gratified now to see the flow of energy and outbreaks of colour along the street that was named for him, from the strawberries and peaches of the early-morning marketers to the silk and lipstick of the late-night clubbers.

The painter Charles Hill was a central figure in the artistic life of colonial Adelaide. Some critics are lukewarm in their assessment of his skills as a painter – his formal training was in engraving – but there is general accord about his empathy with his fellow-creatures: his interest in human warmth and feeling and the representation of those qualities on canvas, and in conveying emotional expression and connection. The Proclamation painting, says one critic, 'emphasises the cheerful domesticity of the gathering', which in the case of some of the colonists it certainly does, but other faces there seem the opposite of cheerful. Colonist Margaret Stevenson, who with her fellow passengers had found it hard to bear Governor Hindmarsh's autocratic selfishness and oblivion to other people's comfort on the voyage out and was now not impressed with his insistence on a little pageantry in the hot sun barely hours after they had all disembarked, noted in her diary that 'during the whole of the ceremony not a *Buffalo* face, at all events, was to be seen unwrinkled by a frown or not distorted by a sneer. Sad, sad, this!'

Aware of the written accounts and able to talk with many who had been there that day, Hill would have been very alert to the emotional tenor and temperature of the event, as he was in all his work. In a very different painting, 'The artist and his family', for instance, there's a complex emotional narrative. On the surface it's a peaceful family meal, but you can see very clearly the emotional currents and undercurrents running around this large family as the children grow and change. On one side of a table set for a meal, three more or less adolescent siblings sit in wooden self-consciousness, ignored by their parents and glumly watching the action across the tabletop: their mother is adoringly nursing the baby, their father is being cuddled round the neck by the toddler, a little sister is sitting at her father's knee and a little brother is half under the table tormenting the family dog. A sharp-eyed servant girl has just arrived with a platter of golden summer fruit. They are seated in a sort of veranda or patio, with vines growing up the trellises and a view, in the background, of a clear blue sky meeting the familiar purple horizon line of the Adelaide Hills – which may or may not be a deliberate visual joke but which is, either way, a fitting backdrop for a family portrait of the Hills, of Adelaide.

Among the original colonists were three gifted amateur artists: young solicitor John Skipper, Governor Hindmarsh's daughter Mary and Colonel Light himself. These three provided the earliest images we have of the first days and weeks and months of the colony, and their work appeared together in 'Exhibition of Pictures: the Works of Colonial Artists', the colony's first group show, in February 1847. In their recording of Adelaide's earliest population and development as a city, they were later joined by others, including the prodigious watercolourist S.T. Gill and the gifted and witty Martha Berkeley, Adelaide's first professional female artist. But the colony's growing culture of visual arts was disrupted, as were so many other aspects of Adelaide life, by the discovery of gold in

Victoria in 1851. Catherine Helen Spence's 1854 novel *Clara Morison*, part antipodean *Jane Eyre* and part feminist utopia, is a detailed depiction of the way much of the male population went scampering off over the border with stars in their eyes on the hunt for something sparkly, while the women stayed at home, hewing wood, drawing water, learning self-reliance and keeping the colony going. It was mainly Charles Hill who revived the artistic life of Adelaide, after he arrived in 1854.

At the age of 30, and on the recommendation of a senior churchman, Hill had emigrated from England to South Australia in 1854 in the hope that its dry climate would aid his recovery from tuberculosis. While the weather hadn't worked in this respect for consumptives Harriet Gouger and Colonel William Light, and indeed in both cases had only intensified their sufferings, Hill was luckier; he spent the rest of his life in Adelaide, living to 91 and seeing the colony folded into the Australian federation.

Arriving in Adelaide less than 20 years after it was surveyed, he quickly became a central and busy figure in its artistic life. Newspaper ads and articles of the day show him teaching art at St Peter's College, the oldest and still the most sought-after and expensive school in Adelaide, as well as setting up a business in engraving and portrait-painting in King William Street and teaching private art classes four nights a week in his home in Pulteney Street. He was a central figure in the establishment of the South Australian Society of Arts in 1856 and remained active on its committee for many years. 'The Society of Arts still holds on its way,' reported *The Advertiser* on 12 December 1870. 'Every year it seems to gather new strength, to present fresh novelties, and to take a firmer hold on the public mind.'

Investigating this painting and its history, I came to see Charles Hill as one of those people whose enthusiasm and momentum are infectious: as far as the artistic life of colonial Adelaide is concerned, he can be discerned by about 1860 as at the centre of a critical mass which he himself had likely built and nurtured. One 19th century historian of 'Notable South Australians or Colonists' recounts – in the passive voice so beloved of his time – Hill's centrality to the city's growing interest in the arts:

> Having inaugurated a School of Art at his own residence, preliminary meetings with a view to increase its usefulness were held, and a society to

promote its interests formed. It was not, however, till 1860 that the School of Design, of which this was the nucleus, was opened, with Mr Hill as master.

It's possible to trace the origins and growth of the city through the late 1830s and the 1840s through the works of the earlier artists, and a feature common to many of their works is the skyline to the east: its gentle undulations change colour with the changing light, but its outline does not, and to contemporary Adelaideans that high eastern horizon, anchoring the composition of the Proclamation painting as it does that of so many others of the period, is immediately recognisable, felt as one of the boundaries of home. No matter where you are in Adelaide, you can always see the Hills; put any Adelaidean in front of this painting and even one who doesn't know the story of the Proclamation or the Old Gum Tree will know the horizon line. One of the paradoxes of this painting is that to those familiar with the topography and the history, the place is clearly Adelaide in spite of the fact that Adelaide didn't yet exist. The vast 14-exposure 'Panorama of Adelaide' produced 30 years later by photographer Townsend Duryea is a comprehensive image of the whole rapidly spreading city, taken in a complete 360-degree circle from the scaffolding on the uncompleted tower of the Town Hall, but to a contemporary Adelaidean, little looks familiar – though few of us have seen the city from this angle – and it's hard to connect with this photograph until you come to the images taken towards the southeast, where the gently rising line of the Hills and the bump of Mount Lofty immediately tell you where you are.

The odd sensation that the pre-embryonic Adelaide of the Hill painting looks somehow more like today's Adelaide than the burgeoning city of the much later Duryea photographs leads to questions about the nature of authenticity versus the power of imaginative truth, for even now, in the era of digital photography, with its easy manipulation, a photograph still has a status level of accurate documentation that nobody could ever claim for a painting. Yet we know that a drawn or painted portrait will often reveal things about its subject that no photographer, no matter how gifted, would ever be able to capture.

So the contemporary eye, habituated to the photographic documentation of historical events, finds Hill's painting problematic. Knowing that it's a painting of a historic occasion, the brain wants to read it as an image captured in real time. The people in the painting really existed and were really there on the day in question, doing what they appear to be doing in the painting; the site is real, the horizon instantly recognisable and the remains of the tree are still in place today. So the brain wants to believe that the picture tells the truth: perhaps not quite that it's a photograph, but that it has a photograph's function, provenance and veracity.

Charles Hill indeed saw his role as partly that of a recording historian, and it was important to him that the Proclamation painting should be an accurate record of the event, even though it took place when he was still a child in England. That Hill was not present has been given by at least one art historian as a reason for not trusting the painting's accuracy. Another observer says that the painting 'presents an Agatha Christie type of mystery', pointing out that it was signed and dated twice by the artist, once in 1876 and again in 1881, with the later signature partly obliterated, and that there are two keys to the painting, with the first, Hill's own original list of names, clearly having been altered. George Sierp's 1940 key to the painting is different again.

There are other anomalies. Governor Hindmarsh is shown wearing the uniform of a Rear-

Admiral, a rank to which he was not actually promoted until 1856. Robert Gouger, in his journal, identifies the flag that was raised as the navy's white ensign, but in Hill's painting the flag, though still partly furled on the ground, is clearly identifiable as the Union Jack. And the distinctive arched-over trunk of the Old Gum Tree may not have been the site at which the Proclamation was read after all: accounts by two people who were present on the occasion do not match, and discussion on the subject has raged – intermittently – in the pages of Adelaide newspapers from that day to this. If it wasn't on this site, then the notion that it was is a myth that took hold early: the composition of a photograph taken around 1868 by Adelaide photographers Dailey & Fox showing the tree, with a copy of the Proclamation nailed to the apex of the arch, certainly presents it as an object of significance and mystery. Mark Twain thought so too, when he visited Adelaide in 1895: 'As I approached it seemed bent with age and possibly with discouragement and despair, but as I came nearer I saw a perfect arch – a symbol of strength and perpetuity.'

But the painting's most significant mystery is the figure at its centre, standing between and slightly behind Governor Hindmarsh and his proclaiming private secretary, George Stevenson, and lined up between the Proclamation document and the peak of Mount Lofty at the painting's very heart. This central figure wears the British Army's uniform: white breeches, black hat, and a red coat against which the white page of the Proclamation document in Stevenson's hands shows up brightly. He is easily identifiable, from the several other portraits and self-portraits of him that exist, as Colonel William Light. In the original key to the painting, that name has been written in and then altered to 'Colonel William', though there was nobody in the colony by that name. In the 1940 key, the names and identities have been juggled some more, with no further reference to anyone called William or Light.

There's a simple explanation for this tortuous history: Light wasn't there. On the arrival that morning of Governor Hindmarsh aboard the *Buffalo*, Light's deputy, George Kingston, had been sent to fetch him for this ceremony. But Light, who had already been delayed in his task and who knew there would be more trouble when the new colonists discovered that they had, as yet, nowhere to live, refused to attend what his biographer Geoffrey Dutton calls 'Hindmarsh's little circus', preferring to stay, like Achilles, in his tent, and get on with the task for which he had been employed. Letters written in 1980 to the then Director of the Art Gallery by two of Hill's grandchildren give conflicting accounts of this mystery, but the more convincing one states that the Art Gallery had initially refused to buy the picture on the grounds that it was not historically accurate, including, as it did, the portrait of Light. Hill had been urged to change the picture but had refused, saying, 'If he was not there, he should have been.'

What makes this picture valuable? Artistic merit? It has limited value as a work of art. Historical accuracy? It's been established that the painting isn't a fully accurate representation of the events it depicts. The importance of the occasion? Much as cultural memory holds this to be the 'birth of South Australia', the colony had come into being the previous February, on the issuing of the Letters Patent.

Yet in 1936, the Art Gallery of South Australia was willing to part with the not inconsiderable sum of £157 10s 6d in order to acquire Hill's painting, and to provide the substantial amount of wall space it took up. Was this sentiment, or nostalgia, or an understanding that history and cultural memory are not necessarily the same thing, but that both are important? Or was it simply a response to the best thing about the painting – the variety of human feeling discernible there – and to its undeniable emotive power for Adelaideans who can see in it not only the beginnings of Aboriginal dispossession but also the courage and trepidation of this little group of settlers in a strange land? Margaret Stevenson had noted in her diary 'the smallness in number of the new people, the vastness of the plain around them'.

Whatever it was, this painting was created to mark a momentous occasion for the colonists, and to remind Adelaide of its first civic and ceremonial gathering. Hill began the painting in 1856, aiming to record the moment that Adelaide's city-hood, as a lived reality, began: it was an act of memorialisation. Perhaps the Art Gallery's purchase of it in 1936, the centenary year of South Australia, was another. It gives us a point of connection between the present, in all its unremarkable familiarity, and the past in all its unrecoverable strangeness.

4

The Statue

Colonel William Light is an Adelaide folk hero. His statue stands high on a hill overlooking the city, his body is buried in the city square that bears his name, his image appears on postcards in every postcard stand at every newsagency and every tourist trap in town, his birthday is celebrated every year in a well-attended public ceremony, and his is the only body that has been legally buried within the city square after settlement. He became an official part of his city in a more literal way than any other European has ever done, and his name has become almost synonymous with it. The restless young man in Paul Kelly's song 'Adelaide' sings *I own this town, I spilled my wine at the bottom of the statue of Colonel Light.* And most people who grew up in Adelaide know exactly what he means.

The statue stands in a flowery little parklet dedicated to it on Montefiore Hill in North Adelaide.

Made in 1906 by the Scottish sculptor William Birnie Rhind, it's a life-size bronze figure but looks larger than life because of the unusual height of the pedestal, which already seems elevated because of its position on the hill. Dressed in military garb, holding a rolled-up map in one hand and pointing out across the city with the other, the figure looks poised and alert and full of energy from every angle.

Light is remembered as the man who drew up the plan and chose the site of Adelaide, and who then surveyed its streets and the 'town acres' that were ready to be sold and built on: as the man who had the good taste and good sense first to site the city on a river running through such a beautiful part of the coastal plain, and then to design it as a set of rectangular grids fitting snugly along and around the topography on both banks of the little river, really more of stream (and in the driest months barely a creek), that the colonists named the River Torrens, after Colonel Robert Torrens, and the Kaurna people called Karrawirra Parri: 'Redgum Forest River'. Torrens was the original chairman of the Colonisation Commission that oversaw the establishment of the colony and one of the men who, with the help of Governor Hind-marsh, made what was left of Light's life even more of a misery than it already was. On a plaque on one side of the statue's granite pedestal there's a passage from the journal that Light wrote in the last year of his life, after many of his papers and records and the personal journal he had kept for 30 years were destroyed in the fire that burnt his hut to the ground:

> The reasons that led me to fix Adelaide where it is I do not expect to be generally understood or calmly judged of at present. My enemies however, by disputing their validity in every particular, have done me the good service of fixing the whole of the responsibility upon me. I am perfectly willing to bear it, and I leave it to posterity and not to them, to decide whether I am entitled to praise or to blame.

The 'enemies' to whom he refers were various. There were the Colonisation Commissioners back in London, who hadn't given him enough time to find a site and survey the city before the colonists began to arrive, who kept pushing him from London to hurry up, who refused his request for extra men to help with the surveying work, and who finally demanded that he abandon his trigonometric survey for the faster but less accurate 'running survey', a last straw that saw him resign from his post in 1838. And much closer to home there were the colonists who complained with increasing bitterness that they had nowhere permanent to live, and the people who had set their faces against the site he had chosen for the city.

Chief among these was Governor Hindmarsh, who was smarting under the doomed system of shared power that saw him and the resident Colonial Commissioner, James Hurtle Fisher, constantly at odds. The situation made Hindmarsh, an autocrat by nature, even more pushy and touchy about the limits of his powers, and obliged all the other city officials to take sides, which made life particularly hard on Robert Gouger as Colonial Secretary and more generally meant that in any disagreement the other officials and colonists lined up in tribal opposition. In addition, Hindmarsh was a British Navy man and was obsessed with the notion that the city must be sited at a deep-water port; he favoured Port Lincoln and Encounter Bay (both dangerous for shipping) as well as Port Adelaide (which had no supply of fresh water) over Light's choice, whereas Light regarded the fresh water supplied by the River Torrens as more important and thought the that the good deep-water port six miles (9.5km) northwest of the city was quite close enough. Once the city had acquired bullock wagons and bullocks to pull them, so that colonists and their belongings could be easily transported to the city and fresh water could be transported to the port, this was indeed the case, but by this time Light had won the fight simply by going ahead with the survey in the spot he had chosen.

But perhaps Light's biggest ongoing problem was Hindmarsh's private secretary: George Stevenson, the black-clad civilian in Charles Hill's Proclamation painting who is holding and reading out the document. Stevenson, a well-educated Scot, seems by all accounts to have been an intellectually gifted but very nasty piece of work, someone who used his good brain to connive and manipulate and stir up trouble apparently for the sake of doing so. He was supported in his Machiavellian behaviour by his formidable wife Margaret, and he had considerable influence over Hindmarsh. Stevenson encouraged Hindmarsh in his resistance to Light's choice of site for Adelaide, and the latter makes it clear in his 'Brief Journal' of 1839 that he was fielding criticism from all quarters; on the one hand there were the disgruntled colonists who wanted him to make them a city and be quick about it, and on the other hand there were people – notably Stevenson – inquiring publicly why he hadn't taken *more* time in choosing the site, why he hadn't made an exhaustive exploration of the coast and countryside before making a decision. 'The clamouring emigrants and the ignorant, despotic Governor,' say Light's biographers, who are nothing if not partisan, 'were converging on him while delay was piling on delay. His cry to the Commissioners is as true as it is futile: "I ought to have been sent out at least *six months* before anybody else!"'

Attacks on Light were not confined to his lifetime. Architectural historians Donald Leslie Johnson and Donald Langmead published a book in 1986 arguing that it wasn't Light who chose the site and designed the city at all, and that the credit for both achievements should go to his deputy, the 'uncouth', 'haughty', 'ungentlemanly' and 'incapable' Irish republican George Kingston. The truth probably lies somewhere between; one of the interesting things about this debate is its fixation on the idea that the origins of Adelaide must be attributed to one man and only one man. In order to decide which man, one version must be accepted and the other rejected, for, in Light's and Kingston's written recollections of events, each –

perhaps pardonably – sees himself at the centre of the action.

Johnson and Langmead do have a case, however, and what seems most likely is that Light and Kingston, working together with a team of men and using various templates for city plans, going back to Ancient Greece, and including Italian Renaissance designs and the layouts of Philadelphia and Savannah, arrived at consensus about where and how the city should be set out, and that Light as the person in charge was the one who got the credit. Certainly Light's contemporaries give him the credit – including those who opposed him, wanting the city sited elsewhere, and thought that what was due to him was not credit but blame – and it's equally certain that it was Light alone who met and bore the weight of this opposition, and successfully held out against it. Johnson and Langmead seem to be ignoring the plentiful evidence in the letters and journals of his contemporaries, notably Robert Gouger and Light's own assistant, William Jacob, that Light was the driving force in the siting and surveying of the city.

Part of Johnson and Langmead's case is that Light was too ill to have done the hard physical slog of exploring and surveying. When he first arrived in

South Australia he was already 50 years old and far from well; he was asthmatic and consumptive, tormented by the heat and worn out by walking everywhere, for in the earliest days of the colony there was 'not a single horse, pony or ox' to carry any of the colonists or their equipment, though Gouger and Hindmarsh (and probably others) had brought smaller animals – goats, pigs and dogs – with them from England. It's certainly true that Light's state of health sometimes held up his work, and he died of tuberculosis, embittered and bereft, less than three years after he first arrived in the colony. The elaborate sandstone cross that Kingston designed as a memorial for his gravesite in Light Square quickly wore and weathered away, and was replaced in 1905 with the monument that still marks the grave today: a tall column of red granite supporting a surveyor's theodolite, which makes an odd but intriguing memorial in the middle of the square's high ground. But the legend of Light had grown between his death and the turn of the century; the committee that had agitated for a new memorial wanted a separate statue as well, and in 1906, after 14 years of delays, planning problems and financial problems, the statue was finally erected in the middle of the middle of town, at the very centre of Victoria Square.

Over the next three decades the statue gradually became a traffic hazard, hemmed in by vehicles and tramlines and overhead wires. After some public fussing it was finally moved in 1938 to a small balustraded park at the top of Montefiore Hill, on the corner of Pennington Terrace and Montefiore Road in North Adelaide. From this vantage point at the edge of the parklands on the northern side of the River Torrens, Colonel Light seems to be looking back across the river and down over the city, proudly pointing out its beauties.

North Adelaide is a place of large and handsome 19th-century buildings: churches, hospitals, university colleges. As a lifetime non-resident, my own sense of it is haunted by these buildings and my experiences in them: a hallucinatory week in the winter of 1957 as a very sick small child in a chilly, bleak, high-ceilinged ward behind the Dickensian façade of what was then the Adelaide Children's Hospital; a hot evening in 2003 singing carols with the Adelaide Philharmonia Chorus in St Peter's Cathedral; and a drive through the broad empty streets and the still, warm air in the small hours of the morning, sometime near the end of 1970, in the passenger seat of a Mini-Moke owned and driven by a sweet and sober dark-haired boy from

St Mark's College who took me up to his room for no more dubious purpose than to give me his copy of *The Hobbit*. And if he is reading this, I want him to know that while I may have forgotten his name, I remember his hair as it was on a midsummer's night in 1970 and almost certainly is no longer: curly, and abundant, and black.

Mostly, though, the college boys regarded themselves as out of my league, having been taught – or at least some of them had – to avoid the girls from state schools at all costs. (I'm told by Adelaideans currently in their early 20s that whenever you go to a party, the first question anyone asks you is still – just as it was 40 years ago – 'Where did you go to school?') North Adelaide is full not only of imposing institutions but also of large, luxurious private houses, indicating that here is one of the places where you'll find a high concentration of Adelaide money. The pursuit of that money in the world of commerce, however, is mainly confined to the central thoroughfares of O'Connell Street or Melbourne Street; the residents, if not strolling there, are sitting in their big offices, or their beautiful houses, or their large well-tended gardens. The little park built around Light's statue is at the top of the road that sweeps from the city across the river and up Montefiore Hill, on one corner of a broad, quiet intersection where everything seems big and old: the stone walls are high, and the dark trees cast abundant shade as their roots erupt up through the footpaths. Traffic can get a little busy on this corner at certain times of day, but there are few pedestrians. Misleadingly, this park is called 'Light's Vision'; given the height of the hill and of the granite pedestal on which the statue stands, he is towering over the city and can certainly see a great deal, but the place where the flesh-and-blood Light actually stood to fix the site and begin the survey is near the corner of North and West Terraces. A modest plaque in stone and bronze marks the spot, and major roadworks and the development of the new hospital have so far left it carefully unmolested.

William Julian Light was born in Kuala Kedah in what was then Malaya on 27 April 1786, just over a year before the First Fleet set sail. He was an illegitimate son of Martinha Rozells, a Eurasian woman of Malay and Portuguese (or possibly French) parentage, and Captain Francis Light, himself an explorer and adventurer in the name of empire. Light was sent to England at the age of six to be brought up by a family friend; his father died in 1794, and his guardian died in 1798, when he was 12. Back in Malaya, his father's former friends were busy cheating Light's mother out of his inheritance (though that is a murky story whose details are not clear) while his guardian's widow in England tried to decide what to do with him. Light had fallen in love with the sea on the voyage to England as a little boy, and so at 13, after a good education in which he had excelled at languages and drawing, he found himself at sea in 1799 as a 'volunteer boy, 3rd class'.

Light spent the next 15 years in his country's service. After six years in the navy, he travelled to India for his sister's wedding and spent some time there; his biographers, Dutton and Elder, speculate that his hopes of gaining a position in the East India Company were thwarted by its negative attitude to mixed-race employees. So he joined the British Army, and fought Napoleon's forces in Spain under the Duke of Wellington; in an 1828 history of that war, we get a glimpse of the sort of character he was:

Lord Wellington was desirous to know whether
a small or a large force thus barred his way, but
all who endeavoured to ascertain the fact were
stopped by the fire of the enemy. At last Captain
William Light, distinguished by the variety of his
attainments, an artist, musician, mechanist, seaman
and soldier, made the trial. He rode forward as if
he would force his way through … but when in
the wood dropped his reins and leaned back as
if badly wounded: his horse appeared to canter
wildly along the front of the enemy's light troops,
and they thinking him mortally hurt ceased
their fire … He thus passed unobserved through
the wood to the other side of the hill … and
ascending to the open summit above put spurs to
his horse and galloped along the French main line,
counting their regiments as he passed. His sudden
appearance, his blue undress, his daring confidence
and speed, made the French doubt if he was an
enemy, and a few shots only were discharged, while
he, dashing down the opposite declivity, broke
from the rear through the very skirmishers whose
fire he had first essayed in front.

By 1823, Light was fighting in Spain again. In
1821, in Londonderry, he had married a woman
about whom nothing is known but her surname,

but she apparently died within two years. Back in combat he was shot in the thigh and severely wounded by a musket ball, so he was shipped home from Corunna by his guardian's widow, the aptly named Mrs Doughty, with whom he had stayed in touch. The following year he married an acknowledged beauty by the name of Mary Bennet, the illegitimate daughter of the Duke of Richmond – and the opposite of her namesake, the plain piano-playing middle sister in Jane Austen's *Pride and Prejudice*, in every possible way. Together they spent the next six years travelling and living in the Mediterranean; having spent much of his time in the army sketching the terrain, Light now spent much of this time drawing and painting the European cities and coasts, which was to stand him in good stead when it came to assessing the lie of the South Australian land 10 years later.

In 1830 the Egyptian ruler Mohamed Ali drafted him into the service of the fledgling Egyptian Navy as a recruiting officer, but while he was away on this mission his beautiful and wilful wife became involved with another officer, for whom she eventually left Light, taking all of her own money and some of his. For the second time in his life, he had been cheated out of a large sum of money, so when offered the post of Surveyor-General to the planned new colony of South Australia he accepted, grateful for the prospect of a salary. He eventually sailed for Adelaide on the *Rapid* with a young woman half his age called Maria Gandy, who was unable to marry him as he was still technically married to Mary, but who remained his companion for what was left of his life.

After less than two years in South Australia at the service of the Colonisation Commissioners, in which time he had completed the survey of Adelaide and begun surveys in surrounding districts, Light's dealings with them, frustratingly delayed by the slowness of the voyages carrying the mail, had become intolerable to him: 'My disgust and hatred now of all that has transpired makes me sick of serving and I hope soon to be my own master.' The contrast between the attitude and behaviour of Light's 'enemies' and those of the friends and co-workers who supported him in Adelaide could not have been greater; at a dinner given in his honour barely two weeks after he wrote of his 'disgust and hatred' in a letter to Colonel Torrens, the resident Commissioner was moved to observe in a Dickensian tribute that 'if the combination of every thing that was honorable, every thing that was gentlemanly, coupled with extraordinary talents, centred in one man, that one person was him on whom you have bestowed a testimony of your regard'. Light was too overcome to reply, and after a couple of attempts to do so, contented himself with proposing a toast: 'The labouring classes of this colony.'

After his resignation Light formed a small private company with Boyle Travers Finniss, a member of his original surveying party, and continued to work. He was living with Maria in a reed and thatch surveyor's hut between North Terrace and the river, with Finniss in a similar hut nearby, while his brick house was being built at Thebarton, near the river. One hot January day in 1839, a fire broke out in the Finniss hut and quickly spread to Light's; both were burnt to the ground. The fire took all of Light's drawings and paintings and the personal journal he had kept for 30 years. All these things had been packed up, as the household had been due to move to the new Thebarton house within a few days. His health declined rapidly after this, though he continued to make a little money through his drawings, and by acting as adviser to the surveying company. On 6 October 1839, aged 53, 'he died cared for by a woman he could not marry, in a city he had founded but could not live to enjoy'.

But by some alchemy of cultural memory, even his moments of extravagantly bad luck have become part of the charisma that hovers in a rosy cloud around the figure of Light. Gifted in languages, painting and music as well as in the physical arts of war, intellectually sophisticated, good company and naturally skilful at almost anything he tried, he was both a Renaissance man and a child of the Enlightenment; and fraud, betrayal, rivalry, scandal, fire, assorted wives and lovers, military battles, extensive and adventurous travel, conflict with the Queen's authorities and a finally a fatal disease all conspire to make him seem not just a Romantic hero but a Byronic one to boot. Johnson and Langmead are right to argue that his life and personality were 'the very stuff of which myths are made', but it doesn't follow that the myth has no substance behind it. There must have been some good reason why Light was held in such high regard by most of his fellow colonists, why 450 mourners followed his coffin from Holy Trinity Church to his grave in Light Square, and why, when the first monument at the gravesite weathered away, the city council saw fit not only to replace it but to put up a commemorative statue in the centre of the city as well.

The statue of Light is one of only a few life-size realist statues of real people in Adelaide that capture the imagination and make the passer-by stop to wonder who this person might have been. The city contains monuments to three British monarchs, but they look static and uncompelling, as was perhaps required by the dignity of the monarchy; the bronze statue of Queen Adelaide clad becomingly in her riding-habit, situated in the Town Hall, is both more modest and more charming than any of the monarchs in the streets. Queen Victoria remains in the middle of the square that bears her name, where she has been since she was unveiled in 1894. Part of what's now a muddle of clashing symbols there, she would have stood tall on her pedestal in Edwardian Adelaide but is now dwarfed by the tall flagpoles flying the Aboriginal and the Australian flags high above her head, by the tower of the nearby St Francis Xavier Cathedral, and, on the opposite corner, by the Adelaide Hilton. The Law Courts around the western and southern sides of the square make a more fitting and dignified backdrop for a 19th century English queen.

Victoria ascended the throne in the same year

that Adelaide was surveyed, on the death of her uncle King William IV. For 30 years she shared her position in the middle of the square with the statue of Light, until the latter was moved to North Adelaide. If the mind's eye zooms out far enough to take in both of them at once, and follows the direction of Light's pointing finger, it can see that Victoria and Light look as though they are having a conversation. The fat little bronze queen, well into middle age, gazes sternly north from her vantage point in the exact centre of the city, while Light, energetic and commanding in his military garb (and looking a great deal younger and healthier than he actually was by the time he arrived in Adelaide), pointing imperiously south-southeast across the river, gazes back at her. With a mile of hot blue Adelaide air between them, they regard each other steadily: over the river, over the heads of the cricketers on hot summer afternoons at what used to be the most beautiful cricket ground in the world, over the tops of buildings and trees, over the heads of the streaming pedestrians and the bold bronze and marble explorers – Matthew Flinders, Charles Sturt, John McDouall Stuart – as well as of the stiller, quieter Adelaide luminaries of the intellect also immortalised in sculpture: Sir Mark Oliphant,

Dame Roma Mitchell, Sir Howard Florey, Catherine Helen Spence. Light and Victoria gaze at each other past the branches of eucalypt and willow, past magpies, lorikeets, rosellas and blackbirds, past white ducks and black swans and water-birds of all kinds, speaking to each other of the city that both did so much to establish in its earliest days, Victoria not in person but at a distance by force of empire and its symbology, Light by hard work and personal struggles in the last and most difficult years of his life.

In their statues they look about the same age, the Queen perhaps older, but in life Light was old enough to be Victoria's father. When she took the throne in 1837, less than a year after Proclamation, she was 18 and he was 52. He was by then often ill or exhausted or both, living out the romantic legacy of his illegitimate, racially exotic and adventurous background by cohabiting openly with his loyal mistress, and too sick, by now, to care much what the burghers of Adelaide thought about it. The popular view of Queen Victoria suggests that she would have been deeply shocked by the living arrangements of her faithful colonial servant, but at 18, passionately in love herself, she might privately have held views somewhat different from those traditionally invoked in her name.

Keeping her company in Victoria Square are the statues of two explorers and a former Premier, and of these four figures, only Charles Sturt looks like someone who might come alive. The others were two of Adelaide's most colourful personalities, and yet their statues succeed in making them look static, rigid and uninteresting. John McDouall Stuart, whose statue stands in the northeastern corner of the square, was the explorer who first crossed the continent from south to north, in a nationally valuable expedition that opened up the overland telegraph route. And he returned alive – just – to tell the tale. In the statue he seems overdressed, draped about and cluttered up with symbolic objects: a Union Jack draped over one shoulder, a rolled-up document clutched in one hand and a saddle and sextant at his feet. Stuart was a fey little Scottish elf of a man, small and slight with an intense expression and raddled face, but the statue makes him look stocky, squat and ponderous. He was also, by all accounts, a determined and ferocious loner, a man of implacable will and a heavy drinker, none of which stopped him from spending 20 years in the colony exploring, surveying and prospecting, pushing further and further inland and drawing maps as he went; by the time he embarked on his expedition to cross the continent he was a formidably experienced explorer who knew much of the terrain already.

Manning Clark, in *A History of Australia*, devotes thousands of words to those expensive, incompetent show-ponies Burke and Wills, but his remarks on Stuart, the man who succeeded where Burke and Wills had failed (and the expeditions took place at the same time, with the whole of Australia watching the race to see who would get there first), add up to barely a page – and most of that is very peculiar and repetitive harping, underlaid by a sort of forced joviality, on Stuart's drinking habits. This is the sort of eastern-states-based cultural nation-building that makes Adelaideans sigh and roll their eyes; given the magnitude of Stuart's actual achievements as an explorer, it would have been nice to see them properly recognised in the magisterial six-volume national history.

If Stuart was indeed 'a wild ass of a man', as Clark biblically calls him, then an even wilder and much bigger ass stands across the square: Charles Cameron Kingston, son of George Kingston and Premier of South Australia from 1893 to 1899. He was an overbearing force of nature who played a major part in the process of Federation and became Minister for Trade and Customs in the first Federal Cabinet under Prime Minister Edmund Barton. His achievements as Premier included the establishment of a high protective tariff, the regulation of factories, the establishment of a system of conciliation and arbitration and the granting of the vote to women, making South Australia only the second place in the world – New Zealand was the first – to do so.

His statue looks imposing enough, the life-size figure in its full Privy Council garb with a sword and some nicely carved and very pretty floral embroidery and braiding on the frock-coat, but the person in the statue looks calm, conciliatory and static. In life nothing could have been further from the truth: the *Australian Dictionary of Biography Online* entry for Cameron includes the words 'black hearted', 'courage', 'formidable athlete', 'imbroglio', 'lechery', 'loaded revolver', 'quarrelsome', 'seduced', 'terrible bully', 'titanic ego', 'tyrannical', 'unscrupulous', 'vindictive' (twice) and 'warm and generous friend', though it tactfully avoids the word 'syphilis'. The year before he became Premier, Cameron got into a quarrel with the conservative MP Richard Butler that resulted in his challenging Butler to a duel in Victoria Square, then much bigger and bushier than it is now; Butler sensibly informed the police, who arrived in Victoria Square to find Cameron with a loaded revolver. He was arrested and eventually bound over to keep the peace for 12 months, a ruling still in place when he became Premier. A couple of years later Kingston and his viperous tongue – again in Victoria Square; it seems to have held a fascination for him – so enraged the manager of the South Australian Company that the latter attacked him violently with a riding whip, drawing blood:

> The powerfully built Kingston wrested the weapon away from his assailant and proceeded to chastise him. He later told the press: 'Who can now say that I have not shed my blood for South Australia? What a pity, my capitalistic friends will say, that there was not more of it.'

In a macabre and long-delayed coda to this tempestuous life, Kingston's body was exhumed from Adelaide's historic West Terrace Cemetery in 2008, exactly a century after his death. This was part of an investigation by a brother and sister claiming descent from one of his illegitimate children, of whom there are rumoured to be at least five. Teeth and bone fragments were sent for DNA testing, which confirmed that the man who had requested and paid for the exhumation, Malcolm Simpson, was indeed Kingston's great-grandson:

> Mr Simpson, 61, said his family had always known the former premier was the father of his late grandmother, but that it was important to make sure the legend was true. The main reason he had pursued the genealogical mystery was to vindicate his grandmother, ostracised because of her illegitimacy and sent to an orphanage. 'An eight-year-old girl in an orphanage, who knows who her father is, who knows who her mother is, and neither will have anything to do with her.'

Ever since I began to write this book I've been thinking about the connection between place, identity and lived experience, and have been haunted by the phrase 'the body in the city', in all its possible meanings; I sometimes thought I might be overdoing it, but stumbling across this story in the last stages of writing the book has made me wonder whether, on the contrary, I might not have taken it far enough.

Over in the northwestern corner of the square, the explorer Captain Charles Sturt – who is *not* buried in Adelaide – has been far better served by his sculptor than any of the other figures here. Clean-shaven and simply dressed in comfortable riding clothes and a broad-brimmed hat, shading his eyes with one hand and holding a telescope and map in the other, Sturt looks lifelike, animated and endearing. He was exactly nine years younger than Colonel Light, with an uncannily similar background; more commonly associated with New South Wales, he also made substantial contributions both to knowledge of the inland terrain and to public life in South Australia. He lived in Adelaide from 1839 to 1853, and his home near the sea, The Grange, is still standing and operates as a museum. His success as an explorer was not matched by any gift for political life; although he served in South Australia as Surveyor-General, Colonial Treasurer and Colonial Secretary at different times during his 14 years in Adelaide, and although he was a popular and respected figure, he repeatedly made a mess of his career as a public servant by clumsily offending powerful people. One historian says that 'his capacity for arousing and retaining affection was remarkable; it made him an ideal family man but a failure in public life ... In this sphere he might well be described as a born loser.'

This side of Victoria Square has several cafes on it, and pigeons therefore abound; more often than not, Light has one perched on his hat, having a good look around for leftover bits of sandwich and pie. There's a 20th-century feel about the clean lines of the Sturt statue that suggests photographs of beautiful Edwardian youth along Rupert Brooke lines, perhaps no surprise considering that the statue was unveiled in 1916.

The Sturt statue sculptor, Adrian Jones, had as interesting a life as his subject, and had already provided Adelaide with what remains one of its most powerful, animated and easily recognisable pieces of public sculpture: the South African War Memorial at the corner of King William Street and North Terrace, outside the gates of Government House. Captain Jones was not only a sculptor but also a career army officer and a trained veterinarian who saw active service in various British theatres of war, including the Boer War itself; his best-known work is the 'Peace Quadriga' on top of Wellington Arch at Hyde Park Corner. It is a chariot drawn by four very lively horses and driven by a little boy, with Peace descending on angel wings. As a sculptor Jones was known to be the man to go to if what you wanted was horses, and he pleased the committee in charge of commissioning the sculpture (a group of eminent Adelaideans holidaying in London) by offering to do it faster and more cheaply than anyone else. His South African War Memorial is one of Adelaide's main landmarks, placed on a high pedestal at the corner of a large open intersection where it's clearly visible, as well as interesting and beautiful, from most angles and distances. A huge, powerful horse is being pulled up hard at the peak of a rocky outcrop by a rugged-looking soldier in a slouch hat, peering intently north along King William Road and holding his rifle in one hand as he leans back easily in the saddle, his body following the movements of the horse: he is a figure Jones thought would appeal to 'the sturdy Australian people'. The statue is at once spookily realistic and beautifully designed, full of balancing diagonals and harmonious arrangements of mass and space.

The South Australian Boer War veterans had gone to South Africa as colonial citizens of a British province fighting for England in an imperial war, and had come home, in the wake of Federation in 1901, as Australians. In terms of military history the Boer War was the beginning of a national identity, the first conflict for which troops were raised by the new Commonwealth (though by the time those three contingents arrived in South Africa, the war was over), and the returned soldiers of the colonies formed the nucleus of what was to become the Australian Light Horse. This was Adelaide's first war memorial, and since its unveiling in 1904 it has accrued meanings it didn't have to begin with, in the way that war memorials do; among other things, it's strongly associated with the nearby Torrens Parade Ground behind Government House, from where several generations of soldiers subsequently departed for war.

This memorial has its haunting counterpart on the southeastern corner of North and East Terraces: the Australian Light Horse regiments are memorialised by an obelisk and the War Horse Memorial beside it is an inscribed granite water trough. In contrast to the South African War Memorial horse, which is so very powerfully present, the water trough for horses conjures up their poignant absence, for only one Australian horse ever came home from World War I. The inscription is from the Book of Job:

> He paweth in the valley, and rejoiceth in his
> strength. He goeth on to meet the armed men,
> he mocketh at fear, and is not affrighted, neither
> turneth his back from the sword.

Jones seems less interested in glorifying war than in the dynamics of horse and rider, the fitting-together of human and animal bodies in motion, and what appeals most about this statue, to the ordinary non-military onlooker, is its animation. Something about the paused pose of horse and rider suggests both the movement that led up to this moment and the movement that will lead away from it, just as the statue of Sturt seems to have caught him in mid-gesture. The Boer War memorial is one of three North Terrace statues that have this eerie quality of suspended animation, and the other two are just along from it, in the shade along North Terrace's Prince Henry Gardens outside the Government House wall. Balancing the military archetype, there's the marble copy of Canova's Venus, a delicately poised Goddess of Love looking deceptively vulnerable as she steps from her bath, clutching the classical equivalent of a towel to one perfect little breast while artlessly exposing the other, plus the whole of her slender back and shapely behind, her hair fetchingly dishevelled in what the celebrity trash mags would call an updo. Venus, 'startled as she steps from her bath', is apparently pausing to listen and to hide her naked-ness; like the soldier and his horse, she seems to have just stopped moving, and to be about to start again.

Between the soldier and the goddess, however, is the calm bronze figure of Dame Roma Mitchell, Companion of the Order of Australia, Dame Commander of the Order of the British Empire, Commander of the Royal Victorian Order and Queen's Counsel. She was Australia's first female QC, its first female judge, and the first woman to be appointed Governor of an Australian state. Born in 1913 into a Catholic family with strong regional ties, Dame Roma lived in Adelaide all her life; she graduated in law not long after her 21st birthday, having her photograph taken in an elegant suit and dashing hat at the centre of a group of fellow graduates, and was admitted to the Bar with nine others a few days later, the only woman in the group. She took silk in 1962, and at the instigation of the young Don Dunstan, then the state Attorney-General, took her seat on the Bench of the Full Court in September 1965, whereupon the South Australian press resorted to predictable inanities, asking if she would be called 'Mr Justice' like all the other judges. 'I hope not,' she replied. 'It would interfere with my social life.'

In this witty bronze statue by Jeanette Moore,

Dame Roma sits in a low antique armchair on a solid, modest-sized granite pedestal, which raises her up but keeps her within reach, at a distance from which you could talk to her without raising your voice. Her legs are demurely crossed at the ankles, and one arm rests loosely on the arm of the chair. She is holding an old book closed with her other hand, keeping her place with a finger, and there are more old books in an untidy pile at her feet. Loose bronze sheets of paper blow about the pedestal; most of them are blank, but a couple contain information about the statue and on a third is inscribed the Mitchell family motto, *Sapiens qui assiduus*: 'He is wise who is industrious.' The statue has a quality of stillness that is paradoxically full of life, for in it Dame Roma is doing what she did best: listening and thinking. Head tilted, gaze shrewd, she appears to be sizing up whoever she is listening to, relaxed yet ladylike from the neck down, but from the neck up attentive, with a raptor's intensity.

Neighbours in the deep green shade along the Government House wall, both life size, Venus and Dame Roma seem to be the presiding female deities of the city. Both have dainty little feet that would easily fit into the fragile black silk slippers, with embroidered royal crests on the toes, that once belonged to Queen Adelaide and are now displayed in the Town Hall. Venus in her white marble and Dame Roma in her black bronze seem the two faces of womanhood, the Odette and Odile of North Terrace. But this notion, appealing as it is, falls apart pretty quickly: the bronze Dame Roma cannot be the treacherous, lawless and ruthlessly seductive black-clad Odile of *Swan Lake* when everyone knows it's actually the goddess Venus who is the embodiment of all such dangerous womanhood, and looking at Venus's pretty feet, messy hair, faux shyness and shapely bare bum, you have to admit that she in no way resembles the virginal Odette. If the juxtaposition of these two along the terrace makes it inevitable that they be paired and compared, then perhaps we need to work with a different mythology: Dame Roma is Minerva, goddess of wisdom, and Venus is simply herself.

Also captured doing what he did best in life, further down the road in front of the gates to the Adelaide Oval where the seasonal tidal waves of cricket fans can see him as they pass, is a bronze Sir Donald Bradman, left foot well down the pitch, bat in the air like a weapon, hitting his trademark cover drive. As with Venus and the Boer War soldier, it's the sort of statue that irresistibly suggests the movements that came before and after this moment, and draws the observer in to imagine them. The sculptor is South Australian artist Robert Hannaford, best known for his revealing, insightful portraiture. 'The Don' was unveiled in 2002:

> Hannaford found working on this sculpture
> exhausting … showering at the end of a
> working day he instinctively began scrutinizing
> his own body in the mirror, twisting his head
> and shoulders to better understand the way the
> muscles and bones and limbs behaved in the act of
> wielding a cricket bat.

These four figures – two real, two allegorical – are the Adelaide statues you can most easily imagine coming alive at midnight, stepping down from their pedestals like Hermione in *A Winter's Tale* and getting together to compare Adelaide notes. Sir Donald and Dame Roma, born only five years apart, each of them sophisticated, civilised and musical, might share a stately, well-executed waltz down North Terrace, but allegorical personages are rowdier and less inhibited: the soldier would probably just scoop the willing and near-naked goddess onto his horse and retreat with her to some secluded stretch of the river bank in the dark, as so many have done before.

Life-size realist statues of real people have about them a whiff of the uncanny. They are a way of perpetuating someone's physical presence beyond death, like a mummy, or a ghost. A statue is an effigy, a doppelganger, a voodoo doll. Seeing one defaced can be distressing; watching one topple can induce a shiver in the soul. They wield their enormous power partly through paradox: a good statue is motionless by definition yet somehow suggests movement. The giants of a city's life can be easily forgotten over time, but good statues like those of Sir Donald and Dame Roma and Captain Sturt and Colonel Light himself, statues that don't just memorialise but inform and re-enliven the memory of their subjects, can keep those people in our gaze and continue to make them part of the city's identity, as they were in life.

In the days and nights immediately following the end of World War II in August 1945, the streets of Adelaide were packed with people cheering and dancing and kissing. One journalist with *The Advertiser* captured a moment when two Adelaide icons – the horses of the Mounted Police, and the favourite Adelaide meeting-place of the period – came together in an image of singular sweetness: 'At the Beehive Corner two white police horses had Victory Vs and other symbols drawn on their noses with lipstick. Never in Adelaide's history have so many bylaws been broken by so many people with so little retribution.' At night the city was flooded with all kinds of lights after long years of blackouts and privation:

> … in Victoria square floodlights lit up the surroundings like day … From Montefiore Hill Adelaide looked like a fairy city. Coloured neon lights, searchlights, flood lights, rockets, Roman candles, and the headlights of motor cars threw a great lurid glow against the sky. Dominating the whole scene was a giant illuminated V …
> In both city and suburbs there was also a glow from stained glass windows in churches where thousands offered up prayers of thanksgiving for peace.

Up on Montefiore Hill the fireworks were lighting up the sky, and on the night of Thursday,

16 August 1945, professional Adelaide photographer Keith P. Phillips, who had fought in both World Wars, was celebrating in the crowd. But he was also working, and he took what remains one of the city's most beautiful and startling photographs. 'Pyrotechny', a black-and-white photograph taken from about 10 metres away and facing west, shows the whole statue of Colonel Light, including the tall pedestal. Behind the statue, fireworks explode and soar; using a long exposure time, Phillips captured their movement and showed them up as trails of light across the night sky, intricately embroidered with starbursts. At the bottom of the photograph you can just see, from the outlines of their heads, how dense the crowd is, milling around at the base of the statue, with their faces upturned to watch the fireworks. 'Hundreds of rockets shot through the sky, weaving delicate smoke trails, and showering red, green and white stars …'

A bronze statue on a dark night would be invisibly black on black, but against this fiery background and the softer glow of the illuminated city, the statue of Light appears in clear, sharp silhouette. He seems, with that pointing finger, to be drawing a trail of light in the sky. In its stillness and its paradoxical capture of moving light, the image recalls, in a strange half-inversion, an early historian's view of Light's brief time in Adelaide: 'Like the swallow in the Anglo-Saxon legend, he flashed from the darkness across the firelight, and out into the darkness beyond.'

5
The Rotunda

Small children, when they are in that enchanted phase of learning to speak, will often fixate on a particular word and repeat it to death before, to the relief of their exhausted parents, moving on. Some words are more voluptuous than others, giving pleasure to mind and mouth; one such little boy of my acquaintance particularly enjoyed the words 'elbow' and 'Kalgoorlie', and a favourite word of my own as a small child was 'culprit', which would seem not to bode well for adult life. But I once knew a toddler, the nephew of a friend, whose taste in repeatable words marked him immediately as a child of Adelaide: he was briefly transfixed by the word 'rotunda'.

The rotunda in question is a real one, an elegant octagonal late-Victorian bandstand, crafted in Glasgow and in 1881 shipped in pieces to the Adelaide City Council, who re-sculpted the entire southern bank of the Torrens Lake near King William Road in order to make a flat and elevated surface for it in an open part of Elder Park and then put it together piece by piece. The donor, Sir Thomas Elder, had accomplished this by fiat; he simply wrote to the Council while he was away travelling in Scotland saying that he had ordered the structure and it was on its way. The *South Australian Register*'s report on the proceedings of the council meeting in August 1881 quotes his letter:

> Having noticed in the last batch of Adelaide newspapers that the Torrens Dam is now drawing near completion, and that it is the intention of the City Council to beautify the banks of the river … as a place of recreation and a promenade, it occurs to me that the occasion would be a fitting one for presenting the Council with a rotunda or band stand, and I have ordered one to be made and sent out to the colony without delay; and I take the liberty of asking you, in the name of the Council, to accept it as a token of the interest which I, as a temporary absentee from the city, still feel in its affairs.

The Torrens Dam to which he refers is the weir that was built in 1880 to dam the river and form an ornamental lake, which solved a number of problems, including the effect that 40 years of settlement had had on the river: in its original state the Torrens had been a pretty stream lined with tall trees, but it was now not much more than a denuded and smelly swamp. 'If there was one topic which was liable to make the mid-Victorian champion of Adelaide shuffle his boots with embarrassment,' says historian Peter Morton, 'it was the condition of the River Torrens.' The construction of the weir and creation of the lake solved some problems but caused new and potentially worse ones, including the silting-up of the lake. The Torrens can dry up to a sad little trickle in summer, but it has a large catchment area in the Hills and some of its watercourse is very steep and narrow, so after heavy rains it's liable to flood – that needed to be managed as well. After long delays, the weir was finally rebuilt to a new design in 1928 and the worst of the river's problems were solved.

By November 1881 the rotunda had arrived: 'The band rotunda presented to the city by Sir Thomas Elder has arrived in the colony, and tenders will shortly be called for its erection on the esplanade. We believe the structure is a most handsome one, and no doubt the gift will be thoroughly appreciated by the citizens.' A year later, after a great deal of work on landscaping, foundations and surrounding granite steps, the rotunda was officially opened on a balmy November evening, on which the citizens of Adelaide were treated to a rendition of the 'Rotunda March', specially composed for the occasion and dedicated to Sir Thomas:

> A gala night was arranged by the mayor …
> Happily the night was very fine, and by 8 o'clock,
> the time for the opening ceremony, the esplanade
> surrounding the rotunda was crowded with
> sightseers to the number of at least 3,000 …
> Processions of boats, each illuminated with lamps
> or Chinese lanterns, looking like glowworms on
> the shimmering surface of the water, moved to
> and fro. The flotilla had on board the members
> of the Liedertafel, whose well-trained and
> melodious voices were wafted over the river in
> tuneful harmony. Across the river, tempered by
> the evening breeze, the music was heard to the
> best advantage, and along the favourite walks the
> people who could not find room on the esplanade
> had a delightful promenade and a foretaste of
> the pleasure to come from the open-air concerts
> which are now in course of organisation.

Elder was a well-educated, well-travelled Scottish colonist who made a lot of money in his adopted South Australia as a pastoralist and businessman and gave it away almost as fast as it poured in: most of it to education, music and art. One of the largest sums went towards the founding of the University of Adelaide. He left a bequest to the South Australian art gallery – then a constituted body with a modest collection but no dedicated building – of what would in today's money be over $3 million 'for the purchase of pictures only', an inheritance that finally prompted the government to construct a proper, purpose-built art gallery; the opening in 1900 of the Art Gallery of South Australia was a direct result of Elder's bequest.

The rotunda is over seven metres in diameter, with a domed cupola, a canopied roof and cast-iron railings, all intricately worked but filigree rather than fussy, and delicate rather than ornate. It was repainted in its original colours as part of the South Australian sesquicentenary celebrations of 1986, its details picked out in pale but luminous golds and blues. The land it sits on has been built up at a strategic point in the irregularly shaped park so that it's visible from King William Road and forms a natural focus from every angle of the park, and from the river; it seems to pull that whole part of the city together. An octagon is the perfect crossover point between a square and a circle, between curved lines and straight; the word 'rotunda' names roundness, yet it has eight flat sides. In the visual tension set up between Adelaide's straight streets and square corners and the irregular curves and roundness of the river, the octagonal shape of the rotunda is like a lovely compromise, providing a halfway point where the lines of street and river might be brought into some kind of visual alignment or truce. It's the most beautiful place in the city.

Since 1882, when this structure was first completed, generations of Adelaideans have come to Elder Park for concerts, fireworks, Adelaide Festival opening nights, Carols by Candlelight, open-air celebrations and spectaculars of every kind, more often than not with the rotunda as the focal point of proceedings. And generations of adults and children have gone for walks in Elder Park along the Torrens Lake, where the rotunda catches the eye from every point, and where they can keep a respectful distance as the bossy black swans jaywalk across the winding bicycle paths, intent on stealing some napping office worker's lunch from her or his very briefcase. I have seen it done. There are photographs.

It's a place where many Adelaideans have been happy: where they have gone specifically in order to be happy, and have not been disappointed. My own memories of Elder Park include rolling sideways down its grassy slopes as a child in 1961; snogging with my first-ever boyfriend on the river bank one Saturday afternoon in 1967; sitting on the balcony of a bar in the Festival Centre with a gin and tonic and listening to Boz Scaggs rehearse over at Memorial Drive one hot dusk in 1978; drinking champagne with a friend when on a visit home from Melbourne in 1987 and watching the red and yellow paddleboats reflected upside down in my champagne flute in the sun, as the condensation ran down the sides and left trails of moisture through the image, and thinking 'I really must come home to Adelaide'; walking along the river's edge with a visiting Melbourne friend after I had indeed come home, some time around the turn of the century, as her daughter and her nephew — both 14, fair and fey — clowned around in a bright blue paddleboat in the middle of the river. And there was a soft, warm evening in March 2006 when a handful of old friends and I were among the 30,000 people who streamed into Elder Park as the sun went down, armed with rugs and wine and picnic suppers, to watch a spectacular outdoor night-time show with a beautiful name – *Il Cielo che Danza*, The Dancing Sky – that had been imported from Italy for that year's Festival of Arts: giant balloons with sweet Leonardo da Vinci faces, delicate flying ballerinas, an airborne piano, stories, music, white paper lanterns and coloured lights on the water.

The civic rhetoric around the rotunda at the time it was installed leaned heavily on the pursuit of pleasure. Much has been written about Adelaide's 'nobly depressing rectitude' – its wowserism, its Dissenter-dominated Sabbatarianism, its narrow-minded Philistinism – but you'd never know about any of that from the way the Mayor and the newspapers talk in the 1880s about how wonderfully pleasant it is to stroll down to Elder Park on a hot evening and smoke a cigar while you listen to a good concert. By 1914 there are women writing outraged letters to the paper about the number of young lovers on the banks of the Torrens who are brazenly lying on the grass where decent folks can see them – why, she asks, do the police not make them sit up? – and by 1924 a wonderful new pleasure toy has arrived in Elder Park: the Floating Palais.

The Floating Palais was exactly what it sounded like: a dance-hall on the water, supported by pontoons and moored on the south bank of the river opposite the rotunda. It had two storeys, seating, a refreshment buffet and a 100 x 45ft (30.5 x 13.7m) dance floor. *The Advertiser*'s report of its opening night on 6 December 1924 is a little ambivalent: 'If the public had any doubt as to the stability of the floating Palais on the Torrens, the opening on Friday night provided a good test, as the weather was exceedingly boisterous.' The writer does not elaborate, merely going on to describe in exhaustive detail the colour and fabric of the 'costume' worn by each lady present, but it must have been an entertaining sight: surely a floating dance-hall in exceedingly boisterous weather would beat any Methodist-built sloping floor hands down when it comes to tricky dancing. By 20 December, *The Advertiser* was much more enthusiastic: 'Dancing even on the hottest night, is robbed of its strenuousness when indulged in at the Floating Palais. There are few cooler spots in Adelaide …'

But it's not until the following summer, when the Palais re-opens for the season having undergone some refurbishment over the winter, that the paper gives a detailed description:

Outlined in scarlet and blue lights, which cast long streamers of fantastic colour on the water, with a powerful arc lamp on each of the cupolas which surmount it, and with smaller arc lamps throwing a white radiance from a dozen different quarters on the flat roof, the Floating Palais on the Torrens presented a beautiful appearance on Wednesday evening ... From the City Bridge the Palais looked like a huge Chinese houseboat, and the glimpses caught of the swaying figures of the dancers gave a vivid touch of life and colour to the scene. At closer quarters the effect was that of an Aladdin's Palace ... The interior decorations follow out the Oriental scheme, and terracotta and blue are the prevailing colours, with gilt pillars lending an added touch of richness to the scene.

The Palais continued for a few more years to be a popular success, but in 1929 it was found that the timbers had rotted below the waterline, and no one was prepared to put up the amount of money needed to fix it. Like a dragonfly, it had a short but glittering life.

Perhaps part of the excitement generated by the Floating Palais came from its potential for danger; at least one young lady performed so enthusiastically on the dance floor one night that she disappeared right over the side and had to be fished out of the lake. How many of the dancers were aware of the little river's dark history? For the first 20 years after the creation of the lake, a police building was maintained on the bank for the purpose of housing an officer whose duty it was to fish out the drowned corpses of suicides and the victims of accident or murder.

In 1972, almost 43 years after the demise of the Floating Palais, a man who had been in the country for only six weeks but who had already gravitated to the gay beat on the river bank was thrown into the Torrens by 'a person or persons unknown', and drowned there. And 80 years before the Palais opened, when the colony was only nine years old, an eloquent citizen signing himself 'Humanitas' had written to the *Register* proposing the provision of ropes and poles on the river bank for the purpose of rescuing the drowning:

> Many lives have been lost in the Torrens …
> Whilst I write there are amongst us parents
> weeping for their children. The Torrens is

uncertain, dangerous, and deceptive; its ever varying fords are on the brinks of its fatal depths; he who sinks into one of its dark caverns, finds his passage upwards obstructed by sunken logs and branches, and by projecting banks, and is rarely able to emerge without assistance. The Torrens has had victims enough.

But however sinister its undertow, the river and the park have continued to attract crowds of citizens throughout the city's history: to concerts, fireworks, rallies, and the annual Carols by Candlelight concerts. The first of these was held in December 1944 and drew 50,000 people, a fact that *The Advertiser* reported on Boxing Day in a tone of subdued astonishment:

> Fifty thousand people celebrated Christmas Eve in Adelaide by attending the carol festival held in Elder Park in aid of the Adelaide Children's Hospital and the Somerton Sick and Crippled Children's Home.
>
> Adelaide has never before seen such a great gathering at night ... Long before the festival began all the 30,000 admission programmes (£1,500) had been sold, and thousands of people unable to obtain one gave a donation at the gates,

and sang carols from memory … It gave the city
a Christmas scene of unique size and setting.
Elder Park on the banks of the Torrens was solidly
packed with sitting people … By 6 o'clock they
were beginning to arrive in thousands … They sat
outside the light cast from the band rotunda and a
platform that had been built in front of it for the
orchestra and 100-voice choir. The platform was
lined with 7 ft. candles and floodlit from below.
The orderliness of the crowd was remarkable.

Adelaide had had a long, strange war. Though far
away from the action – or at least so it seemed –
it was emotionally vulnerable and exhausted, with
its sons and some of its daughters away in uniform and its full share of depleted families whose
husbands, brothers, lovers and sons would never be
coming home. At night there had been the black-
out ritual: in 1942, when my father was a teenage
schoolboy, he was recruited as part of a troop of
boys who rode their bikes around the suburbs after
dark, knocking on the door of any house that was
showing a light and politely reminding whoever
answered the door to close their black-out curtains.
Roma Mitchell, at this time a young lawyer, had
volunteered as an air-raid warden in the city streets,
and arrived home one night to see a window in her

own flat glowing with the light she had forgotten to switch off before she left home. Radio 5KA was closed down in 1941 because it was suspected of broadcasting in code to the German boats that were known to be in Australian waters, and while its sending the code to the enemy seems unlikely, the enemy was certainly there. One of these boats had mined the sea approach to Adelaide, in both Spencer Gulf and St Vincent's Gulf, and so was responsible for two of the first war casualties on Australian soil: in July 1941, one of the mines washed ashore at Beachport, south of Adelaide, and exploded as it hit the beach, killing two of the sailors who had been sent to investigate it. The war came much closer to Adelaide than many people know.

So it may have been that as yet another sad wartime Christmas approached, Adelaideans wanted more than usual to feel a sense of community, to go somewhere pleasant and do something positive and uplifting that had nothing to do with the war. Whatever it was, the scene described in 1944 gives some idea of what Elder Park meant to the city – it remained a beautiful place to assemble and celebrate in quiet solidarity for the benefit of children.

6

The Bucket of Peaches

The bucket of peaches is an amalgamation of imagination and memory. That there were peaches in containers is not disputed. I am sure that I remember a particular bucket made of chipped white enamel, the chipped parts black, the white with a tinge of blue. The wooden handle spun like a spindle on its wire arc, a handle carefully turned and shaped to fit the fingers of a clutching fist carrying a heavy load. But I may be making it up. My father thinks it may have been a tin bucket. My sister says it was probably an old kerosene tin with a home-made wire handle. We are all agreed that it was not plastic, though for no good reason.

The truth is that it was probably all these things, for there were many buckets of peaches, every summer, and not only buckets of peaches, but old shopping bags of oranges, bowls of plums and apricots, wooden crates of nectarines and cardboard boxes of oranges and lemons. When my grandparents retired from the farm and moved to Adelaide in the 1950s, the first thing my grandfather did was plant a small orchard in his back yard. Once the trees had begun to bear, the further reaches of the long, narrow yard would be transformed every summer into a sea of green leaves, their fat golden ornaments outlined against the blue.

Since this meant far more fruit than he and my grandmother between them could possibly eat, preserve or make into jam (though they did all of these things as well), most of it got distributed around the neighbourhood. He may have planted the trees to set himself a challenge, or just for something useful, in retirement, to do. Neither the climate nor the work schedule of life on the farm would have allowed for the growing of fruit trees when the two most precious resources of rural life were time and water, so for a man who loved to grow things, growing soft fruit and citrus trees – growing trees at all, in fact – would have been both a novelty and a luxury. Or perhaps after a lifetime of annual wheat and barley harvests in hot Decembers, interrupted only by the three years he spent trundling back and forth with the 10th Battalion between the mud of Ypres and the mud of the Somme, it was simply that he couldn't imagine not growing things that turned gold when summer came. Perhaps by then the gold was in the blood.

If we create meaning from reading by relating what we read back to what we already know, then my many encounters in literature over the years with the phrase 'golden apples' in all its manifold meanings and allusions have always been referred back to the image of my grandfather's little orchard in Adelaide's inner southwest. I read of the golden apples of the sun, the golden apples of the Hesperides, the golden apple of discord that started the Trojan War; I see the word 'pomodoro', which is Italian for 'tomato' but translates literally as 'apple of gold'; I read Yeats or Norse mythology or Eudora Welty; and what I see is a bucket of downy, rose-gold, full-moon peaches sitting on the back step in the morning sun at 35 Warwick Avenue, waiting to be picked up and distributed round the households in the neighbouring streets.

The barter economy once flourished in Australian suburbs, as George Seddon points out in his lovely essay on the vanished Australian back yards of the mid-20th century:

> A lemon tree was nearly universal; other trees
> varied with climate – almond trees in Adelaide

and Perth, plums and apples in Melbourne,
choko vines and bananas in Sydney and Brisbane,
a mango in Cairns, figs and loquats everywhere.
For a few weeks, there was gross overabundance
of fruit, and much trading ('I'll take some of
your plums if you take some of my apples next
month').

I don't know whether my grandfather bartered his
golden hoard for things he hadn't grown himself
– tomatoes? cucumbers? certainly not zucchini or
eggplant for him in the 1950s, and probably never
for him at all – or whether he simply gave it all away.
The rhythms of his life had been set in infancy by
the idea of an annual summer harvest, and perhaps
in his old age he needed to keep that pattern going
in order to make sense of the world. Or perhaps,
like so many Adelaideans, he was simply intoxi-
cated by the ease with which it was possible, with
the help of reliable rain and good soil and hot sun,
to conjure abundance out of the bare ground.

The Australian writer Hal Porter, who spent
several years living in Adelaide during World War
II and who was acutely aware of the city's cultural
and societal shortcomings but equally aware of its
real gifts, waxes lyrical on the subject of its horti-
cultural plenty:

> ... the reality of late summer and early autumn
> when Adelaide, more than any place on earth,
> and as simply as pouring tea from a pot, pours
> forth from a lavish cornucopia into gardens and
> parks and markets and arcade stalls a cascade of
> carnations and grapes and melons, guavas and
> Michaelmas daisies and tomatoes, zinnias and
> belladonna lilies and tuberoses, lavender and
> quinces and cumquats and pomegranates, roses
> and roses and roses.

Porter then feels obliged to undercut all this with a far less flattering elaboration: 'This natural opulence is somehow middle class, like a Mrs Beeton dinner-party table ... like the gloves and hats of the women, the self-sufficient statues in the squares, and the wedding-cake façades of the public buildings.' All of which is, sadly, also true. But the 'natural opulence' of the Adelaide Plains was discovered and exploited early, and Colonel Light, as with so many other things, was making the most of it before anybody else. He was, reported Robert Gouger in 1837, 'the most successful of our gardeners; by mixing some of the river-mud with the natural soil, he has produced by far better vegetables than any other South Australian'. Even after only a year of settlement, the Torrens ran murky with the waste of the growing population, and Light would have been well aware that by the time it got to his house in Thebarton on the western side and therefore downstream from the city, the 'river-mud' would make excellent fertiliser.

I realised only when I came to write this book that my grandfather's little orchard perfectly fits the notion of Adelaide as a city at odds with itself, its straight streets and lofty ideals wrestling with the curved, the excessive, the disordered, the crooked, the entropic and the chaotic. My grandfather planted his nine trees in geometric formation, three by three, in lines as straight as rows of soldiers; but precisely because he'd planted them so carefully and tended them so diligently, they responded by overstepping his military lines, overspilling, over-flowing. They bore their golden fruit so abundantly that he had to prop up the laden branches with forked wooden sticks so that the branches would neither drag on the ground nor break off alto-gether. In the soft-fruit season he maintained con-stant vigilance against the mess on the ground that most of us who have lived with fruit trees take for granted – the windfallen, bird-hollowed or simply overripe soft fruit that falls and rots in a matter of hours to a slippery and sweetly stinking mush.

Thinking about all this, I ring my father to pester him again for facts. His recollection is that there was no barter: that my grandfather simply walked around his neighbourhood – a modest suburb on the unfashionable side of town – giving away summer fruit. 'I think it was partly a sort of class thing,' says my father, to my astonishment. 'He knew there were probably a lot of families around who couldn't afford to feed their kids fruit. He wouldn't have trudged around *Beaumont* giving away peaches.' Beaumont is in the leafy east, a place that a certain sort of person would call, without irony, 'one of Adelaide's best suburbs'. The citizens of Beaumont would have been well able to afford summer fruit, but they would no doubt have found it naff, then as now, for people to be walking the streets giving away food to strangers.

There's something odd about this conversation with my father, some elusive discord or wrong note, that continues to puzzle me till that afternoon. Then light dawns: *a lot of families who couldn't afford to feed their kids fruit.* Was this not the prosperous postwar 1950s, the time of stability and prosperity?

From 1938 to 1965, Sir Thomas Playford was Premier of South Australia. His was the longest term of any democratically elected leader in the history of Australia. He was leader of the Liberal and Country League, which of course in Australia means conservative. Pragmatic, utilitarian and personally abstemious, Playford was a cherry farmer from the Adelaide Hills whose attitude to universities was much the same as Governor Hindmarsh's had been to libraries: he couldn't see the point of them. His government established or upgraded the basic infrastructures of 20th century Adelaide and he believed in public utilities and public housing to the point where he was criticised more by his own party for his 'socialism' than he was by the Labor Party in its perennial opposition, but he had no interest in 'frills' of any kind. He was known, not ironically, as Honest Tom. 'In everything except politics he had very simple tastes,' says Adelaide historian Hugh Stretton:

> He was a total abstainer from alcohol, education
> and tobacco. What he believed in was production
> ... It was all very well to despise the rich and their
> ostentatious expenditures, but Playford could
> never see why the poor needed spending money
> either. He wouldn't have them starve, but ... he
> did starve their social services. Old rock piles
> continued as bedlams, orphanages, reformatories,

with little segregation of their toughest from
their tenderest inmates. Abstemious subsidies
encouraged some churches and charities – but not
too many – to go on doing or neglecting what
anywhere else were the standard duties of the
modern state.

One of these Adelaide charities, an important
outfit that baldly called itself the Crippled Children's Association and had been a beneficiary of
that astonishing Carols by Candlelight turnout in
1944, was another of my grandparents' occupa-
tions. Still in existence today, though with a new
focus and under a different name, this organisation
had been formed in the late 1930s to provide support for the children who had been disabled in the
most recent polio epidemic, and it continued to
do so through the worse epidemics of the 1940s
and 1950s. My grandfather understood Playford,
and supported his government; they were the same
age, from the same farming background, had both
been raised as hard-working, God-fearing Baptists
and had come through the same French fires of the
Great War. They even looked like each other. Playford depended for the success of his government
on the support of other people who were like him,
and he was not disappointed; in Adelaide in the

1950s, there seem to have been plenty of them. My grandfather was a card-carrying, paid-up member of Playford's party and I'm quite sure he'd never read *The Grapes of Wrath*. Yet there he was, with his bucket, walking the suburban streets, knocking on doors to offer the gift of summer fruit.

When I returned home to Adelaide to live at the end of 1997, I bought a little house on the low-lying flats near Port Adelaide, barely a kilometre from the place where my grandfather's own grand-parents had got off the boat from Cornwall a cen-tury and a half before. But it occurs to me only now, as I write about it, that in buying a house on a narrow, deep block whose yard had a clear demar-cation between the inner outside and the outer out-side – the inner with paving and two sheds and a clothesline and a compost bin, the outer full of trees that were full of birds – I was unconsciously replicating my grandparents' house, my earliest idea of what an Adelaide back yard was supposed to be like.

I had, of course, known others, not least the big yard of the house my family lived in when we first came to the city in the mid-1960s: it had an old apricot tree, a walnut tree that you could hear the possums playing in at night, the huge fig tree down on the back fence that belonged to the neighbours but by unspoken agreement provided us with whatever grew on our side once the birds had finished with it, a tall, messy Norfolk Island pine planted far too close to the house, and a mysterious strip of rogue bamboo down the back that grew while you watched and threatened constantly to take over the entire suburb, and against which my parents waged endless war.

One's friends' back yards, of course, are always more mysterious and intriguing than one's own. L's father, for example, was a panel-beater, so the focus of their back yard was The Shed, a huge structure that he built after a big win at the races. It was full of things mysteriously automotive, and big enough to have parties in. R lived in an old house on a long narrow block. It had remained unchanged through three generations, with a solid outdoor dunny, an almond tree, an apricot tree and a big shed down the back, crammed with ancient trash and treasure. S was from an Old Adelaide Family and their house was enormous, very old, and full of character and people and good furniture, but their back yard, apart from being bigger than the usual, seemed reassuringly like everybody else's.

But P's house was another world, for P was Greek. Her social life was as limited as those of Greek daughters in those days usually were, so I wasn't often at her house, but I went home with her one hot day after school, and in her family's dark, silent, spotless kitchen she made me Greek coffee in a copper *briki*, taught me to read my fortune in the coffee grounds, and offered me home-made spoon sweets with a glass of iced water. Out the back not an inch was wasted: everything was under cultivation, disciplined and neat. Between the house and the vegetable garden there was the kind of area that my own mother was also gifted at creating, a liminal space between the back door and the back yard that is neither inside nor outside, a patio or a back verandah walled with a curtain of green, in which blinds and vines and trellises and hanging plants collude and entwine to make you think you're inside a room whose walls the eye wants to sketch in, but are mainly woven of leaves and light. P's house had this back verandah space, though it was smaller and darker and denser than the one at our house, and inside it there was, up on a stand, a barrel of home-made wine. Look, she said, look, and turned on the tap, and the purple-red wine splashed prodigally onto the cement and ran back down into the earth to feed the cannibal grapevines growing up the trellis.

These events occur in 1970, at the beginning of the Dunstan Decade. There's a high percentage of Greek and Italian families in Don Dunstan's own electorate of Norwood, and as a tireless campaigner and doorknocker he has been getting to know them well, all through the 1950s and 1960s. Over the next few years, as Premier, he will transform Adelaide's attitude to its Greek and Italian citizens, will make their skilful gardening habits and their beautiful food into desirable and fashionable things. But we don't know that yet. P was born in Greece and has been brought up strictly, as a good Greek girl, in our small Australian city. She is at odds with her family, with herself, and with Adelaide Girls' High, where two or three of the junior teachers still find it appropriate to make loud, disparaging classroom remarks about wogs when half the girls present are Greek or Italian. And because of all these things, she is at odds with Adelaide itself.

So the wine-barrel gesture, overtly intended to show me P's pride in her family's practices of cultivation and care and thrift and abundance and general Greekness, also has in its spectacular messiness a kind of violence, an undertone of defiance and anarchy, an element of crossed boundary and burnt boat. At Rostrevor College, a few suburbs up the road, our contemporary Paul Kelly, himself a quarter wog and Catholic to boot, is also growing up in what is still an overwhelmingly Anglophile and Protestant city. *I own this town, I spilled my wine at the bottom of the statue of Colonel Light.*

It was only after I moved home to Adelaide and acquired a yard and garden of my own, the first I had ever had, that I began to notice the signs of seasons — after 40 years of living by the rhythms of the school and academic year. At first it was a case of realising the magpies were nesting, something that no one inside their territory could fail to notice, and thinking 'Oh, it must be spring', or seeing that plants would die if I didn't water them and it must therefore be summer. But over the first couple of years, I learned to tell first what month it was, and, eventually, what week it was, from what was happening to the garden and the trees, from the appearance and disappearance of caterpillar, lizard and leaf.

This heightened awareness coincided with the realisation that in terms of a changing climate, we were now in uncharted waters. One sweltering day early in the new century, perhaps 2001 or 2002, I went outside in the late afternoon – the heat still enough to feel like a full-body assault, as though one had been hit by a rogue wave or the concussive force of an explosion – to see what havoc had been wrought in the yard, and noticed several splotches of bright green in the dust bowl that the yard had become. Something green on the ground was, at this point in the summer, a novelty. I went in for a closer look.

They were dead birds; the brightly verdant splotches I had seen were the delicate, feathery undercarriages of rainbow lorikeets. They had simply fallen dead, splat, from the sky. The official temperature that day reached 43.7° Celsius, or 110.6° Fahrenheit. This was very rare for the Adelaide Plains, and yet it seems like nothing now, only a few years later, when the temperature has been known to reach 47°C. On the worst days, the heat seems to be actually attacking you, pouncing and striking like a wild animal. On the worst days, you go out into the sun and feel the skin on your arms begin to burn.

Of course it can get this hot, and worse, in other Australian cities. But Adelaide heat has two special qualities. One is its longevity: it can go on, and on, and on, with no relief, unbearably, for over a week – the official heatwave record is 15 days. The other is its thirsty, antiseptic dryness: here on the edge of the desert with the humidity so often at zero, it's easy to feel that you are being gradually dried out, desiccated, mummified. Historian Peter Morton and environmentalist George Seddon have both pointed out that although Adelaide thinks of itself as 'Mediterranean', the Mediterranean is quite a large sea, and the northern-hemisphere city closest to us in latitude and climate is not Florence or Aix-en-Provence, but Tangier.

Seddon, who as late as 1994 had still been nostalgically singing the praises and mourning the passing of the traditional Australian back yard on the traditional quarter-acre block, was writing by 2006 of the urgent necessity for Adelaideans to adapt (and this two years before the terrible summer of 2008–09, when the River Murray almost died and the prospect of running out of water began to look frighteningly real): to redesign the city and to re-conceive the way we live. He suggests containing the sprawl, building higher-density housing, and transforming the Parklands into less thirsty urban spaces like the Royal Gardens in central Athens, 'essentially a shady grove of close-spaced trees like the olive, the carob, loquat and arbutus ... But there is no grass and no need of supplementary water.' If we do not radically reduce and rethink our water consumption, Seddon warns, then here on the edge of the desert, at the end of the river, Adelaide may simply die of thirst and become a ghost town: 'Adelaide should be thinking Tel Aviv, Gaza, Tangier – its latitudinal, climatic and natural resources equivalents.'

Morton makes a similar geographical point in his account of Adelaide's milk supply in the 19th century before there was any regulation:

In 1878 the conditions under which milk was produced and supplied to Adelaide were, in the absence of any effective refrigeration or pasteurization, hazardous in the extreme. There was a cultural factor here. Adelaideans lived in a climate similar to that of the countries of North Africa and the Middle East; countries which sensibly and traditionally used olive oil or ghee [and] yoghurt and whey. But Adelaideans, stout northern Europeans by origin, insisted on their liquid milk, their butter and their cream; and they allowed them to be produced by the dirtiest practices. These practices originated in England where the cold weather made them tolerable some of the time, but they proved downright lethal in the hot dusty climate of Adelaide.

On the day in December 1836 when the Proclamation that brought the colony into existence was read, the temperature was recorded as 103° Fahrenheit. For anyone of my generation or older, this way of thinking about the summer temperatures – 'century heat' – has never quite faded away; perhaps there's some form of onomatopoeia or other sense-association in the fact that 'a hundred and three' has more syllables than 'thirty-nine'. It's a heavier, a *hotter*, thing to say.

Whatever the reason, the words 'a hundred and three' conjure up for me a set of precise and detailed memories of the dry and dazzling Adelaide heat. It's 1969 and my friend L and I are 16. We are hooning up and down the steep and winding roads of Belair in the Adelaide Hills in her FJ Holden, our bare legs sticking painfully to the molten front seat. Now it's 1970, and I pass out neatly and quietly, head on desk, for 10 minutes in the middle of the Year 12 French exam, conducted in an oven-like transportable classroom with no air-conditioning, before being revived with some water by a flustered teacher who'd thought I was just having a little rest. Then it's 1975, and the early-morning picnic party in Botanic Park for my friend R's birthday sees almost everyone sunburnt and drunk by 10am. *A hundred and three.*

And then it's 1980, and I am on the epic journey that so many ambitious young Adelaideans must take, the journey out of Adelaide to test ourselves somewhere bigger and more difficult, something the Kaurna people also know. *Yertarra padnima taingiwiltanendadlu*, says the stone sculpture at the entrance to the Festival Theatre: *If we travel the land then we become strong.* I don't know it yet, but I won't come home to live for 18 years. It's a night-time train journey at the end of Valentine's Day and the February heatwave has continued for over a week, exhausting everyone beyond endurance; today it's a hundred and three again and the Adelaide Hills are on fire. The train surges east through the evening, and out of the window I can see the glow on the horizon, and sometimes I can see the flames. I have forgotten to bring a book; thank God for the Gideons. I sit in my air-conditioned sleeper, drinking wine and reading the Song of Songs and the Book of Revelations, and the Adelaide Hills burn.

Three years later, almost to the day, I emerge with friends from a Melbourne restaurant after dinner, the heat in the street still sucking the breath out of us, and we see that large black flakes of something are drifting down from the sky, which makes no sense. It is Ash Wednesday, 1983, but we have been at work all day and don't yet know what has happened to our corner of the country. I go home to watch the mid-evening news on TV and the first words I hear are 'Adelaide is ringed with fire.' I spend the rest of the evening trying to call my parents, who live in the foothills, but I cannot get through. All around the southeastern coast of Australia, nobody can get through to anybody, nobody knows if anybody is alive or dead. My family is fine, as it turns out, but many people are not, and as I dial my parents' number over and over again, they have already heard on the radio something that will quickly pass into Adelaide folklore: journalist Murray Nicol, describing in a live broadcast what he can see in front of him:

> I'm watching my house burn down. I'm sitting
> out on the road in front of my own house where

I've lived for 13 or 14 years and it's going down in
front of me. And the flames are in the roof and –
Oh, God damn it. It's just beyond belief. My own
house. And everything around it is black. There
are fires burning all around me. All around me.

Summer in Adelaide: the nourishing and the
destructive golds, the soft fruit and the fire. As in
other parts of the country, bushfires in Adelaide
are by no means new, but between the water restrictions and the scorching heat, the old-fashioned
fruit-and-veg culture of the Adelaide back yard is
getting harder and harder to maintain, just as people
are becoming newly conscious of its desirability.
The rains of 2010 gave many Adelaide gardeners
relief, but they will not save us from whatever the
longer term will bring.

Over the last few summers the city has had
severe water restrictions, though in the wake of a
much-wetter 2010 these were eased. The drought
conditions over the last few years and what seemed
to be the death of the River Murray have seen
many Adelaideans install mechanisms for recy-
cling grey water, and put in substantial rainwater
tanks to be plumbed through to the house; the
state government is in the process of building a
desalination plant, though there are many problems

associated both with the plant and with any sort of reliance on desalinated water. When things dry up again, at least the citizens of Adelaide will be a little better prepared than they used to be, and a lot more thoughtful about waste. But the weather is less and less predictable, and fruit trees need a lot of water. Over the last few summers there's been a new problem: once the temperature gets very far over 40°C, it starts to scorch the fruit and burn the leaves. Part of my daily household routine in summer, these days, is to go outside in the early morning and anchor a piece of shade cloth over the lemon tree if the forecast maximum temperature is over 39°C. *A hundred and three.*

On such a day the morning chores also include putting out fresh water not only for the birds but also for the lizards. I have done this ever since the November 2006 heatwave, when I heard some loud rustling at the back screen door and went out to find a couple of large blue-tongues waddling up and down the length of the doormat, nosing at the bottom of the door, trying to get into the house to find the water they could smell. Reptiles are cold-blooded, at the mercy of the day, their blood warmed by the sun. I wondered how warm their blood was that day, as they rustled busily round and round the bristly doormat; how hot does a lizard have to get before it boils itself and implodes? Salamander, firedrake: are lizards not born of fire? Were these two not, literally, in their element? The much-loved Adelaide author and educator Colin Thiele, of *Storm Boy* fame, once wrote a book about a bushfire and called it *February Dragon*.

My grandfather lived in South Australian farming country for 60 years, in a place where blue-tongues abounded and the annual rainfall was 50mm lower than it was in Adelaide. He saw a few droughts and a few terrible summers. But if lizards had ever come to his city doorstep begging for water, he would have known it for what it was: a sign that his little back yard paradise might soon be lost.

7
The Photograph

In the week between Christmas 1965 and New Year's Day 1966, we left the farm for good and moved to Adelaide. My parents and my older sister did the work of packing; my younger sister and I, at 10 and 12, were deemed too young to do anything much apart from get in the way, and were packed off on Boxing Day to the Adelaide grandparents. Three days later, the day after Proclamation Day, they took us to Glenelg beach, where the *Rapid*, the *Buffalo*, the *Africaine* and the rest had sat at anchor 130 years before, and where my sister and I, dangerously stuffed with soft fruit, now ran for the water and swam about with hundreds of other people who'd had the same idea. My long-suffering grandparents sat on a rug on the beach in the late afternoon heat, the tail-end of much the same sort of blistering blue and bleached-gold day that had seen Governor Hindmarsh and his boatload of colonists come ashore in that place.

In the water I was approached by someone I'd never seen before: a dark-haired, hatchet-faced, middle-aged man. He informed me that we were 'playing', and proceeded to 'play' with the new adolescent breasts that were threatening to escape from the confinement of my old pink frilly bathers, a garment that my New South Wales cousins, inexplicably, called a 'cossie'. Whatever it was called, it was now about to split like a chrysalis.

I knew this was all wrong, but I couldn't bring myself to be openly rude to an adult. We had all been warned about 'stranger danger', but since the man was neither offering me lollies nor trying to entice me into a car, this was obviously something else. Several adults – parents, teachers – had given us this warning, but none of them had been quite able to bring themselves to tell us what it was that these strangers wanted, or why they were dangerous. Why I did not at any point connect this man in my mind with the perfectly adequate sex education I'd been given or the forbidden adult novels at home that I'd read on the quiet is something I cannot explain. Perhaps I thought you needed to be married.

Nobody had ever done anything like this to me before. Nobody watching would have seen anything strange; all the action was under the waterline. I got away politely as soon as I could and ran back up the beach to my grandparents, who were sitting like a Henry Moore sculpture on the beach, behatted and resigned, on their sandy tartan rug. But I said nothing about it to them or anyone else. It didn't seem to be anybody else's business. I also felt ashamed, though aware that this made no sense. At that age, when the learning curve gets too steep, you simply shift your weight and change your grip. This, I thought, must be one of the things that happened to you in the city.

And I had learned two valuable lessons. One was to mistrust the motives of any male stranger who approached me. The other was that even when you're out in the open, in the daylight, in the bright water with family close by and hundreds of people around you in the city's oldest and most public place, you are never, necessarily, safe.

A month later, the week before I started high school, three children disappeared from the same place on the same beach. It was Australia Day 1966, the sea and sky glittery with noonday heat and the sand and water dense with holiday crowds. Media coverage and public discussion in the ensuing weeks leaned heavily on those atmospheric clichés that have a hint of the supernatural: into thin air, out of the blue. The children have never been found, dead or alive. Their police file is still open. They were siblings, aged nine, seven and four, who had gone to the beach together on the bus with no accompanying adult, as was not unusual for the times. Their names were Jane, Arnna and Grant: the Beaumont children.

In the days after their disappearance, several photographs of them together were released to the press. To someone of their generation, which is to say my generation, the photos are hard to look at, because they look so very much like anyone's family photos of children from that era: their unknown but clearly dreadful fate could have been anyone's. Of the two photographs that were most widely distributed and reproduced, one is a carefully posed shot of the three children self-consciously sitting on the beach: a generic 'Australian family, 1960s' photograph. But the other looks more specific and more spontaneous, has more life and feeling in it. The children, despite the fact that two of them are wearing identical clothes, look more differentiated from each other, more themselves. And the picture seems to be telling a little story.

In this photograph, which along with several

others of the same three children was reproduced hundreds of times in newspapers and magazines across the country and is now very easy to find online, the two older children, the girls, are dressed in identical school uniforms for summer, of lightweight, light-coloured cotton, with broad straw hats. The little boy is still too young to go to school. Both of the girls are on their tricycles, one with her small school case slung over one handlebar, the other with her bigger case tipped sideways into her bike basket; this older child is laughing. The little boy stands sideways between them, the three of them grouped near the wall of what looks to be an ordinary suburban house. Something about the photograph, perhaps the crispness of the school uniforms and straw hats, perhaps the brightness of the summer light, suggests that this is a first-day-of-school photograph. It seems to be very hot. It's a nice ordinary family photo, of the kind that families took in those days, with an iron rule of amateur photography at the time being observed: that the subjects had to face the sun so their features wouldn't be in shadow, which is why, in so many photos of children from this era, at least one child is squinting grotesquely and at least one more is feebly attempting to shade its eyes with a hand.

Hundreds of thousands of Australians born in the late 1950s and early 1960s have old photos of themselves as children, taken in the same sort of place on the same sort of occasion, posed and grouped in the same sort of way. The deep anxiety that haunts us about lost children is not just about losing our own children, but about losing ourselves. If three children can disappear off a crowded beach on a summer's day, then anyone can disappear from anywhere.

But I don't think my stranger on the beach was their stranger on the beach; I must have been so sure of this, in fact, that I didn't even make a connection until I was in my 40s. Whoever abducted and almost certainly killed the Beaumonts – three obviously pre-pubescent children including a four-year-old boy – would not, perhaps almost by definition, have been interested in a 12-year-old girl who looked 15. But another event of a kind so similar that most people assume it's connected to the Beaumont case occurred seven years later when 11-year-old Joanne Ratcliffe and 4-year-old Kirste Gordon disappeared from a football match at Adelaide Oval, near the river, after Joanne had offered to take Kirste to the toilet. Despite numerous reports of sightings immediately after they left the adults in the group, they have never been found either; nor has anyone been charged with their abduction.

But there was a different pathology at work in 1976, when 23-year-old Christopher Worrell and 37-year-old James Miller, who had been in jail together and established a sexual relationship there, took to cruising the streets of Adelaide picking up girls for Worrell, who'd been happy enough to use Miller sexually in jail but once out reverted to the crime for which he'd been imprisoned in the first place, the aggravated rape of a young woman. Miller was homosexual and in love with Worrell, and continued to act as driver and dogsbody after Worrell began, in December 1976, to kill his victims and dump their bodies, mostly in the bush near a little town 80km northeast of Adelaide called Truro. In February 1977, after he had raped and killed seven young women in a little less than two months, Worrell lost control of the car he was driving on a country road and was killed instantly in the resulting accident, as was the woman in the car, who was almost certainly his eighth intended victim. Miller was also in the car. He survived the crash, and two years later told a friend about the murders, which led to the recovery of all the bodies. It's a blackly entertaining detail that he had been christened Christopher Robin. 'He was a weird one,' said a prison officer who remembered him, after his death. 'A bit kinky.'

One of Worrell's victims was the daughter of an Adelaide couple whom many of us knew. Juliet Mykyta's parents, Anne-Marie and Irush, were well known in education, drama and literary circles, by people who had studied or taught with them, or been taught by them. The Mykytas were not only widely known but also well liked: generous, entertaining, clever and good company. In 1981 Anne-Marie published a book called *It's a Long Way to Truro* in which she told the story of Juliet's disappearance and death, putting it into various wider contexts like the good writer she was.

She recalls in the book that not long after Juliet's body was found, she had two very particular phone calls within a couple of weeks. One was from Les Ratcliffe, the father of one of the girls who had disappeared from the football match in 1973, who wanted to talk about the establishment of a formal association for the victims of crime. The other was from a distressed woman called Judy Barnes, whose 16-year-old son Alan had disappeared two or three weeks after the discovery of Juliet's body. A week after he disappeared, Alan Barnes's body had been found dumped under a bridge; he had been drugged, and had bled to death from gross wounds to the anus. Over the next three years, three more bodies were found in the same state, with a fourth too badly decomposed for the cause of death to be ascertainable but otherwise fitting what was all too clear a pattern. The final victim was 15-year-old Richard Kelvin. A man called Bevan Spencer von Einem was arrested in November 1983 in connection with Kelvin's murder, and was convicted of it in November 1984.

A retired police detective who worked on the case, Bob O'Brien, published a book about it in 2002 in which he makes it clear that he and most others working on the case believed all five deaths to be the work of the same person or people, although there was sufficient evidence for a conviction for only one death. There's also evidence that von Einem was not working alone and that a number of people were peripherally involved in the deaths, though no more bodies in this condition were found after von Einem's arrest. O'Brien scornfully discounts the sensationalist speculation, continued on and off for years in *The Sunday Mail*, that something called 'The Family', consisting of well-known Adelaideans in high places, was responsible for the deaths and that its members were being protected by their cronies; there was indeed a 'family', he says, but they were von Einem's 'associates' or 'extended family' within the strange sub-culture of his secret life.

Four months after von Einem's arrest, the Adelaide Festival of Arts began. Writers' Week is a major part of the festival, and in 1984 one of its biggest drawcards was Salman Rushdie, who had won the Booker Prize for *Midnight's Children* in 1981 and was still four years away from becoming embroiled in his own epic of terrifying and deadly weirdness after he published *The Satanic Verses*. A few days before Writers' Week began, there had been a sensational development during Bevan von Einem's committal hearing: he admitted having been in the company of Richard Kelvin on the day he disappeared. Rushdie hadn't been to Adelaide before, but was taking in information about it from the locals, and it was in response to a remark by one of them that he made his now-famous observation that 'Adelaide is Amityville':

> I hear about the vanishing youngsters. Sixteen-
> year-old girls and boys, disappearing into thin
> air ... Adelaide seems more eerie by the minute
> ... a beautiful woman starts telling me about the

weirdo murders. 'Adelaide's famous for them,' she says excitedly. 'Gay pair slay young girls. Parents axe children and inter them under lawn. Stuff like that. You know.'

Now I begin to understand Adelaide. Adelaide is an ideal setting for a Stephen King novel, or horror film. You know why those films and books are always set in sleepy, conservative towns? Because sleepy, conservative towns are where those things happen. Exorcisms, omens, shinings, poltergeists. Adelaide is Amityville, or Salem, and things here go bump in the night.

If he saw the news of the so-called Snowtown murders trial almost 20 years later, no doubt Rushdie would have felt completely vindicated in his remarks, despite the flak he took from outraged Adelaide locals at the time.

The Snowtown murders, also alliteratively known in tabloid headlines as the Bodies in the Barrels Case, were the last and worst of Adelaide's three separate episodes of serial killings in just over two decades, with 12 murders, torture, cannibalism, dismembered bodies in barrels of acid, all masterminded by a damaged, vicious blow-in from Queensland called John Bunting. All the victims and perpetrators lived in one of the ghettoes of social disadvantage that bad planning and the vagaries of economic history have created in Adelaide's outer northern suburbs: areas that are, sociologically and in other ways, just like the Brisbane suburb of Inala when Bunting grew up. There are ferocious, if straightforward, class-based and gender-based analyses and interpretations of Adelaide's serial murders to be made, but this book is not the place for them.

The strangest thing about Rushdie's comment is that odd skip from psychological aberration to the supernatural between one paragraph and the next. Gruesome murder does not equal haunting, at least not in the way he seems to mean. A violent psychopath is one thing; demons, ghosts and witches are quite another. Rushdie was in a position, if he had taken the murders a little more seriously, to say something psychologically or sociologically interesting about them and be internationally listened to because of who he is, rather than tossing out a superficial joke line and having it land quite wide of the mark. Psychopaths are quite frightening enough on their own; bringing in Halloween effects only muddles and weakens the force of the stories. 'Bump', on the blackest sort of Adelaide night, is not what things go. We have neither ghosts nor witches, at least no malevolent ones that we know of – though some who have visited the Old Adelaide Gaol at night might tell you differently, and the Church of Inclusive Wicca, according to the website of the Adelaide coven Oak & Mistletoe, is an officially incorporated church under the South Australian Associations Incorporations Act 1985.

What Adelaide does seem to have in abundance is what Val McDermid's Tony Hill from *Wire in the Blood* calls 'messy heads': people whose psyches have gone badly awry. The only thing about the serial murders that involved the supernatural in any way was that they led the citizens of Adelaide to ponder anew the question of whether a word like 'evil', firmly located as it is in the discourse of the spiritual and the sacred, and frequently co-opted as it also is by the discourse of melodrama as employed by the tabloid press, could reasonably be applied to behaviour that secular, materialist, non-sensationalist and relatively neutral language would more reasonably describe as sexually aberrant, amoral and criminal.

While the big cities go in for organised crime involving drugs, gangs and guns, and Adelaide certainly isn't free of that, its difference is of a kind that doesn't show up in statistics. The statistics show that crime in Adelaide is much the same as it is in other Australian cities, except for a slightly higher number of reported rapes – and that may be because in a city that has always been good to women in matters of education, suffrage and employment, and where women have historically had a higher degree of influence, power and autonomy than those in other Australian states, perhaps more women are prepared to report rape. It may not mean that the number of rapes is actually higher.

Adelaideans and non-Adelaideans alike could be forgiven for thinking that it was Rushdie who first articulated in print the notion of Adelaide weirdness. But the 19th century versifier Agnes Neale had got in first; in a poem published in 1890, her melodramatic and clichéd language is quite at odds with the sharpness of her instincts:

O Adelaide! we who gaze on thee,
    Entranced at thy loveliness stand;
O beautiful, beautiful city!
    Fair pearl of our bright southern land.
But when night in her dark cloak enfolds thee,
    And the stars burn in glory on high,
There cometh a moan from thy bosom
    That quivereth up to the sky –

Unintentionally entertaining as this may be, and possibly drawing a moan from the reader's bosom that also quivereth up to the sky, it puts its finger on something important. Adelaide is often singled out as the Australian home of weird crime, even in the face of Sydney's own serial killers Ivan Milat and 'granny killer' John Wayne Glover and the brutal torture and murder there of Anita Cobby, or of the Martin Bryant massacre at Port Arthur, or of the unsolved serial murders in Perth, or of the bizarre 'swingers' murders of Maria Korp and more recently Herman Rockefeller in Melbourne. If any of these crimes had been committed in Adelaide, a cry would have risen up in the national media that Adelaide perversity had struck again. Nothing feeds a myth of weirdness like more weirdness.

As I'm thinking about how to write this paragraph, the computer dings to tell me I have mail. It's the afternoon online edition of the Melbourne *Age*, and there's a new headline: 'Stranger Grabs Boy in Bunnings Car Park'. Apparently the 'stranger' tried to lure the child into his car with lollies. I try, and fail, to imagine the jokes there would be in Melbourne (Sydney wouldn't notice) if this headline had turned up from Adelaide. A few years ago when news of a particularly sordid drugs-based

Adelaide murder made it across the border and into the national news, one eastern-states blogger wrote 'South Australia again! Why don't they just run a crime-scene tape right around the border?'

But as Agnes Neale apparently saw, part of what makes Adelaide crime so singular is not so much the crime itself as the contrast between crime – as a concept – and the ideals of its founders, its 'City of Churches' tag, its bragging about its convict-free origins, and the generally goody-goody aspect of its reputation. Against this virginal backdrop, the black oddity of many Adelaide events poses a contrast as stark as day and night: 'But when night in her dark cloak enfolds thee ...'

The Adelaide printmaker and novelist Barbara Hanrahan would have loved this poem, and perhaps did: her own view of the world was starkly dual-istic, though not with any good/evil dichotomy attached. She saw daytime Adelaide as the suffo-cating small-city world of 'proper people' with jobs and hats, and associated 'night in her dark cloak' with freedom, strangeness and art, and with the liberation of her own 'night self':

I emulated my mother and gloated over the Social
Pages of *The Advertiser* ... I conjured up a fabulous
company of doctors' wives in electric-blue Thai
silk and lady-mayoresses swathed in Arctic fox
... At night, alone, I pulled myself clear of the
mediocrities of the world that sought to claim
me. I freed my hair of its restricting pins and it
shivered like a thistle bush.

For the March issue of *The Adelaide Review* in 1988,
due out at the beginning of Writers' Week, the
editor Christopher Pearson – at that stage an influential figure in some Adelaide circles, an independent, fearless and imaginative editor with a strong
literary background, and not yet affiliated with
either the Liberal Party or the Catholic Church –
commissioned from Hanrahan a major article on
the subject of 'Weird Adelaide', intended to address
and answer what she called 'Salman Rushdie's infa-
mous *Tatler* piece'. As Pearson was aware, Hanrahan
had plenty to say on the subject of Adelaide weirdness and the resulting essay is a piece of enchanting
reminiscence firmly grounded in solid, archive-
based scholarship. It explores a different, more
interesting and less murderous kind of Adelaide
weirdness, though Hanrahan was the last person to
shy away from the details of the dark side. Many

– indeed, most – of her novels and prints have a sinister undertone of mystery and sexual threat; it was not by chance that D.H. Lawrence and Flannery O'Connor were two of her favourite writers. But 'Weird Adelaide' is a celebration of the dense yet evanescent material detail of cultural and social history, things lovingly extracted from old newspapers on the basis of their Adelaide-specific oddity, like the elaborate, fragile 19th century Palm House in the Botanic Gardens with its 'moon garden of aloe and agave and cactuses like giant penises and tea cosies and bunny ears', or the 'naughty R rated moulds under the counter (ASK ASSISTANT) in the cake shop in Adelaide Arcade'.

Hanrahan sees the strangeness of Adelaide crime as not unique to the city but rather as highlighted and thrown into stark relief by the contrast with its carefully maintained outer image, which is both of beauty and of virtue:

> The city is so clean, so pretty and so much …
> the big country town that it takes pride in being,
> that it seems, paradoxically, to suit the more
> kinky varieties of evil … And the Torrens, with
> its levelled and lawn-planted banks and picture-
> postcard University Bridge, has had a sinister
> flavour for years. For so many lost girls of the past

in a certain state (which meant an indisposition of several months' standing), those river banks were the place to jump from. And if you did it in a properly weird Adelaide kind of way, you left a confused medley of Scripture texts behind you.

A later and very different sort of analysis involves a similar emphasis on the contrast between the city's public high ideals and the citizens' frustrations and imperfections: Adelaide's second Thinker in Residence, cultural planner Charles Landry, saw in the city what he calls a culture of constraint. There is in Adelaide, he says, 'a sense of trapped energy. A preference for order and perfectionism for which the Light plan of the city stands as the supreme emblem.'

Perhaps he's right, and not only in a symbolic way. Perhaps he's also right in some more literal sense, in which the shape of a city both dictates and constrains the things you will or will not think and do. Some of Adelaide's streets are not narrow, but they are all very, very straight. You would have to make an effort to get lost here, or in any other way to go astray. It seems a town that makes no real allowances for divergence or excess, for irregularity, for ambiguity, for confusion or uncertainty or dissent. Urban landscapes, with their arcades and alleyways, their footpaths and tram tracks, their cafes and shops and signs saying Walk and Don't Walk, are coercive in the way they lure and urge and herd a human body around a city. And if W.H. Auden is right when he says 'the desires of the heart are as crooked as corkscrews', who knows what convolutions and convulsions might be produced by forcing the heart to walk down nothing but straight streets, around nothing but square corners, all of them tending towards a centre that holds nothing beautiful or meaningful for any of its non-Aboriginal citizens, and that it has not chosen for itself?

Adelaideans can quickly find themselves at a loss in Sydney, where the streets are curved and irregular and cattywumpus, turning upon themselves in strange loops, taking you to no one particular place but indiscriminately leading you on to some unknown, unseen and unpredicted end: uphill trudges to seedy dead-ends or jostled crossings to shaded parks or precipitous downhill stumbles to shining waterlines old and new. Sydney, like Edinburgh's Old Town, is itself 'as crooked as corkscrews' and offers unlimited scope for the heart's desire to go its own sweet way, but in Adelaide the expression 'straight and narrow' has a literal as well as a figurative meaning. When you fall off the straight and narrow in Adelaide, it's a long, hard fall with a lot of noise and flailing, and you make an awful mess when you land.

The story of the Beaumont children became a sort of starting point for the 'weird Adelaide' stereotype that has been repeatedly reinforced ever since, partly by sensationalist journalism and partly, alas, by a fairly regular new eruption of criminal weirdness. At the time, the children's disappearance was constructed as a monstrous aberration, a disfiguring wound across the face of what had hitherto been a safe and godly city, 'a wonderful place to bring up children'. One particularly popular line was that Adelaide had 'lost its innocence', though anyone familiar with its history knew that Adelaide, like every other city in the world, had never had any innocence to lose. In any case, it was a line that begged the question of innocence's opposite, not specifying whether that was guilt, or knowledge, or experience. The innocence in question was not that of the city but that of the children, and perhaps the reason that particular photograph is the one that seems to haunt us most is that the children here seem at their most vulnerable, though it's hard to say why that should be so. Perhaps it's the uncertain stance of the smiling little boy, barely out of toddlerhood. Or perhaps it's the tricycles: even the oldest of those three children was still so young that she had not yet graduated to a two-wheeled bike.

8

The Pink Shorts

22 November 1972 was the day the first American
B-52 was shot down by enemy fire over Vietnam.
On that day Ezra Pound was three weeks dead;
Toni Collette was three weeks old. Eight days earlier, the Dow Jones Industrial Average had closed
above 1000 for the first time in history. Indira
Gandhi was the Prime Minister of India; Mao
Zedong was Chairman of the Communist Party of
China, a country then embroiled in the upheavals
of the Cultural Revolution, and to which Republican President Richard Nixon had travelled earlier
in the year for a historic meeting with Mao to re-
establish a diplomatic relationship between China
and the United States. On 7 November, Nixon had
been returned to power in a landslide Presidential
election; conservative politics held sway in the
United States as they did in the United Kingdom,
with Sir Edward Heath firmly established at

No. 10 Downing Street.

In Adelaide, it was already a very hot day by the time business hours began. At the city's biggest and busiest intersection, across from the pedestal where the South African War horse and rider guard the gates of Government House and look out commandingly over the traffic, and just up King William Street from the site of the recently demolished City Baths, where my father used to go swimming as a schoolboy in wartime, in the cool marble halls of Parliament House the leader of the South Australian Labor Party and Premier of South Australia, the Hon. Donald Allan Dunstan QC, was about to turn up for work.

Twenty years earlier, when Dunstan had just won his first bid for preselection, the old-school Labor stalwart Clyde Cameron had taken him aside and told him that if he wanted to succeed as a Labor politician he must do two things: broaden his slender shoulders and get rid of his plummy private-school accent. Dunstan refused to do anything about the latter: 'I said, "Clyde, I have spent years and my parents quite some money on voice training. I'm not going to waste it."' But he agreed about the shoulders, and after a lecture from his doctor in 1959 for working too hard and not getting enough exercise, years before going to the gym became fashionable, he had made it part of his routine. It was having the desired effect, which was one of the reasons why, by the time he became Premier, he was both fastidious and fearless about what he wore.

And so, on this very hot November day, as was his custom, Dunstan arrived at Parliament House wearing tailor-made clothes. But these clothes were new, and the tailor had made them not just to Dunstan's own measurements but to his own design as well: a close-fitting, short-sleeved, round-necked, silky white garment that was a t-shirt in all but fabric and styling, and a pair of tight, brief, deep-pink shorts.

For most of us, the clothes we wore in the 1970s have long since become landfill, or cleaning rags, or patchwork quilts, or children's dress-ups, or bedding for animals at shelters, or have simply broken down into smaller and smaller shreds and patches until they turned to dust. But Don Dunstan's pink shorts still exist, held by a private collector from whom they were borrowed by History SA in 2008 for an exhibition. In his memoir, *Felicia*, Dunstan devotes more than a page to the pink shorts, and concludes that he 'shall bequeath them to the South Australian Archives as a monument'.

In a photograph of them that was used to publicise the exhibition, they look as though they have
never been worn at all. They may well have been
worn only the once: Dunstan recalls in his memoir
that after seeing the furore they had caused, he
put the shorts away. It seems unlikely that anyone
else would ever have had the nerve to wear them:
there's hubris involved in what some would regard
as a blasphemous act, given the status that the pink
shorts have acquired. And having been so precisely
tailor-made for Dunstan, they have about them the
aura of Cinderella's glass slipper, unwearable by all
but one.

They are beautifully made, of a high-quality
fabric, probably some sort of thick cotton. They are
cut so high in the leg and so low in the waist that the
distance from hip to hip is almost twice the distance
from belt to hem. Someone has ironed perfect little
creases precisely down the middle of the perfect
little shortie legs. Dunstan himself describes the
colour as 'a dull rose shade' and says they were similar to the washed-out terracotta pink of a denim in
fashion at the time. One newspaper described them
as 'flesh-pink'. But if the colour of the History SA
photo is true, then they are neither dull nor rose nor

terracotta nor flesh-pink nor washed out: they are richly, heavily, extravagantly pink, the brightly dark colour of a raspberry daiquiri.

There is a more famous photograph, this one rather disappointingly black and white, of Dunstan on the day in question, taken that afternoon and published in *The Advertiser* the following morning to illustrate an article that began with the sentence (the Premier's alliterative name was a gift to journalists and sub-editors) 'Dazzling Don Dunstan does it again'. In this photo you can see that Dunstan looks very comfortable in his self-designed and tailor-made ensemble. His hair, still dark, is windblown and nicely messy, his posture fairly relaxed. He is looking straight into the camera, beaming at it — and, through it, at all the voters who'd be boggling at it the next day. His face is full of fun and complicity, and split by a wide, delighted grin.

A member of the media unit in Dunstan's office at the time recalls the day this photograph was taken:

> … the media already knew that he was wearing them … And we had a very hasty strategy meeting, which took about three minutes, in which we decided that under no circumstances was anybody with a camera going to get anywhere near

Don that day ... We succeeded all day until about four o'clock in the afternoon, when he got out of the office in Parliament House by the back door that we weren't watching and went and stood out on the front steps. And he had quite obviously set it up himself. He *wanted* to be photographed in those clothes.

When I was still in the very early stages of thinking about this book, all the friends I spoke to who'd lived in Adelaide through the Dunstan Decade were lukewarm at best about the prospect of a 'pink shorts' chapter, and some were downright hostile. They argued that to focus on that or indeed on any of the other more sensational aspects of Dunstan's appearance and behaviour was to detract from the significance of his real achievements, which were manifold and major, and had been inspirational and transformative for Adelaide – and, in some instances, for the whole country. My friends had a point, and I wasn't sure about it either.

But it simply wasn't possible to get away from the pink shorts. Almost every book I read that mentioned Dunstan at all contained a reference to them. In an unscientific but nonetheless telling informal survey, I asked a number of friends and acquaintances, both Adelaideans and interstaters, to free-associate when I said 'Don Dunstan', and almost every one of them replied 'Pink shorts!'

The 2008 stage show about him, performed as part of that year's Adelaide Festival, was called *Lovers and Haters*. It was written by Rob George and Maureen Sherlock, playwrights of my generation who had grown up in Adelaide and lived there through the Dunstan years. It had been written not as a musical but as a 'play with music in it', dramatising his rise and fall over the course of the 1970s. A newspaper article about the show in the lead-up to the festival reported that George and Sherlock felt that the pink shorts couldn't be ignored, for much the same reasons that I'm writing about them now. They decided that 'the best tactic was to get the shorts on stage at once, then move on'. At the end of the scene, Dunstan's character says that 'everyone will have forgotten about it by the morning'.

And so the pink shorts were front and centre when the show opened at the Norwood Town Hall, in the heart of Dunstan's old electorate, and the idea of everyone forgetting about them by morning got the biggest laugh of the night. Part of the trouble with the show became evident in the first few minutes, for the costume designer had avoided the extremes of pinkness and shortness that had characterised the real thing, and actor Todd Mac-Donald just did not look the part in this ersatz version; he looked more like a self-conscious non-Mormon modelling the special anti-sex underwear, both unconvincing and unconvinced.

Nonetheless, he bounded bravely about onstage in front of the most difficult audience he could possibly have had – people from Dunstan's time, from his electorate, people who remembered him and had voted for him and admired him and loved him – but MacDonald's high energy and real talent· couldn't disguise the fact that the show was firmly focused on Dunstan's colourful sex life at the expense of his many achievements in social, polit-ical and cultural progress and reform. 'It's just a *cartoon*,' whispered the outraged friend sitting next to me. Dunstan's very old friend Vini Ciccarello, who at the time was the sitting member for his old seat of Norwood and who had helped to nurse him in his final illness, was inconsolable: 'Ciccarello was in tears yesterday as she explained how Dunstan deserved so much better … Having sat, appalled, through the play's premiere, she left as soon as it finished. "I just couldn't bring myself to speak to anyone afterwards," she said.' One excoriating review of the show put its finger painfully on the problem, pointing out that Dunstan had put South Australia 'on the world map as a political powerhouse' and listing some of his reforms and achievements. 'If you paid attention,' wrote Diana Simmonds:

> you might get a teensy hint of this from *Lovers and Haters* but it's more likely that if you know little or nothing of the man, you would think he was a mere dilettante, a trivial publicity hound and a rampant poofter ... The script is an agglomeration of prurient, sniggering piffle that demeans not only its subject but also the audience.

At the end of *Felicia* Dunstan summarises his time in power with two lists: one of his government's achievements, and the other of things it had aspired to but failed to achieve. What's most striking about both these lists is their sheer breadth and variety, but some common themes emerge. Dunstan has been variously described as a Fabian socialist, a libertarian socialist and a social democrat, and many of his government's reforms reflected these labels. On his watch there had been major constitutional reform, and significant improvements in the traditional Labor triad of public health, education and welfare. Workplace reforms were implemented and South Australia now had arrangements for consumer protection and environmental protection. Laws on the serving of alcohol were relaxed and restaurants and cafes flourished, as did the arts, with money going to maintain and develop the Festival Centre and to establish the South Australian Film Corporation. Personal freedom was less constrained, directly and indirectly, by the law. Homosexuality was decriminalised; rape within marriage, on the other hand, was made a crime. South Australia was the first place in the world to enshrine this in law, continuing the state's tradition of enlightened attitudes to women in society, politics and education. As Minister for Aboriginal Affairs, Dunstan was chiefly responsible for the reforms that saw an end to all laws and regulations discriminating against the Aboriginal population, and set up the first-ever legislation, anywhere, for Aboriginal land rights. As he puts it himself, 'Our laws and administration against discrimination on the grounds of race, sex, and marital status also led Australia.'

But the one aspect of Dunstan's achievements

that habitually got the most publicity, not all of it positive, was his active commitment to enabling the pursuit of happiness and pleasure and beauty in the lives of ordinary, individual citizens. The phrase 'quality of life' meant a great deal to him, and a number of his government's reforms were directly or indirectly about the freedom to create and enjoy good food, good wine, good sex and good art to go with the good weather we already had. Dunstan's critics regarded these matters as superfluous and somehow even suspicious, as though the pursuit of happiness were a bad thing, and a focus on the simple pleasures of life somehow the opposite of real, weighty, serious human affairs. But for Dunstan these matters were central not just to the culture of a place but to daily human existence. Not only did *he* give them the attention he thought they deserved; he wanted everyone else to have access to them as well. And in these matters, he tended to lead from the front: he was an excellent (if messy) cook, an avant-garde kitchen gardener, a colourful dresser, a sexual adventurer and a ham in front of a microphone or a camera, and these were the things that most often made the headlines and found their way across the border to the press in Canberra, Melbourne and Sydney.

There are many reminiscences of Adelaide in the 1970s that try in a sentence or a paragraph to take a summary snapshot of Dunstan, to evoke with brevity what he was, *how* he was; among these sketched portraits, the one provided by historian Hugh Stretton – himself an ornament to Adelaide's intellectual life – casts the widest net across the many facets of Dunstan's personality and vision, perhaps because he's writing in the context of Dunstan's passion for town planning and urban design. Stretton, unlike many past Adelaideans, does not dourly regard theatrical *joie de vivre* as the opposite of political seriousness or moral heft. He manages to avoid any reference to the pink shorts, but then can't resist mentioning the gold lamé:

> [Dunstan] himself was not the least of the city's attractions. He wore caftans at home, gold lamé on visits to Melbourne; he read comic verse to audiences at the Festival Theatre and the Zoo, sat on the grass at riverside poetry readings, made intelligent speeches … Some of the staff around him were old beer-drinkers from local government and the party machine; others wrote elegant prose, wore elegant clothes, and divided their favours between daiquiris and campari. Dunstan stood well with both.

With his peacock ways, Dunstan is habitually represented as having brought Adelaide back from a grey wilderness of entrenched conservatism in a triumph of left-liberal enlightenment, but to accept this view unquestioningly is to misread both Dunstan's politics and those of his predecessor-but-one, the monolithic Sir Thomas Playford, Premier and leader of the South Australia's conservative party, the Liberal and Country League (LCL). What most contemporary commentators recognise today as 'left' and 'right' in politics are templates that neither man would come close to fitting. Dunstan, still a hero of the Left, was also a libertarian strongly in favour of individual rights, including the right to privacy, and could be a pragmatic centrist when he chose, while Playford, despite his social conservatism, introduced measures that drew cries of 'Socialist!' from his frustrated party members.

Playford's early life was unforgiving; he left school at 13 to run the family cherry farm after his father had had an accident, and he spent the next six years growing fruit and marketing it in the city. He then joined the army, at 19, and fought in Europe for the duration of World War I. After the war he returned to farming, but with an eye to a political future. He became a Member of Parliament in

1932, and Premier in 1938: he remained Premier until 1965. He was socially conservative, but took a number of economic measures that seemed radical: he involved the state in attracting and controlling industry, introduced price controls, nationalised the electricity supply, built a lot of good public housing and implemented a postwar immigration program, a combination of activities that echoed the colonial aims of Wakefield and Gouger in its balancing of labour, capital and real estate. All of this provided a rock-solid stage on which Dunstan then arrived in the late 1960s to perform his own feats of modernisation, development and reform, particularly in the social and cultural areas that Playford had neglected.

For years before he became the Labor leader, Dunstan had been Playford's chief antagonist in Parliament, pushing hard against the gerrymander – the unrepresentative state electoral boundaries that were keeping the LCL in power. But after a hard day's arguing, Playford sometimes gave Dunstan a ride home to Norwood, and between bouts of parliamentary debate they had some cheerful exchanges, often at someone else's expense; Dunstan's predecessor as Labor leader, Frank Walsh, was an enthusiastic but not particularly coherent speaker, and Dunstan recalls that Playford 'more than once beckoned me from across the House while Frank was speaking. When I had sat down beside him he would say "Now Don, can you kindly tell me what this goat is talking about?" And I couldn't – I didn't know either.'

In Colin Thiele's *The Adelaide Story*, which looks like a coffee-table book but is in fact a solid and accessible potted history of the city illustrated by a superb collection of photographs, there is a shot dated 1972 of Playford sitting at a table and looking up at Dunstan, who is standing beside him and showing him something in a small container or box. They appear to be at some sort of official lunch, which would explain the otherwise inexplicable pineapple in the foreground. Playford is laughing, in a surprised-but-delighted sort of way. Dunstan is smiling. Their mutual affection and respect is clear, as it is in Dunstan's own account of Playford: 'He had a mischievous and impish sense of humour, loved practical jokes, and had no very great regard for some of the more pompous of Adelaide's Establishment.'

Derek Whitelock describes Playford as 'not so much a party man as an individualistic, pragmatic, regional potentate whose first loyalty was to his state and city'. That is also a good description of Dunstan. A friend and fellow Adelaidean, on hearing that I was writing about these two redoubtable Adelaide monuments, sent me a couple of stories about them that were new to me but that seem to sum up the unique qualities of both:

> Dunstan walks into Playford's old office upon his (Dunstan's) election and finds Tom's govt issue pen and battered leather case. Dunstan thought it would be fitting to give them to Playford as a farewell from a grateful SA Gov. Head of Premier's says Honest Tom would feel he could not accept them. Dunstan gets a letter from Auditor General authorising the farewell gift and I think personally delivers them. Tom refused a State Driver in retirement and Dunstan noticed Tom was not attending official functions so sent his own driver to collect him … Oh Adelaide, Adelaide, how I love thee.

My generation came of age during what became known as the Dunstan Decade. For me as for most of my friends and peers, Dunstan was of the parental generation, and in a way we thought of ourselves – perhaps, a little pathetically, we still think of ourselves – as Dunstan's children, which must be profoundly irritating to his three real children, who are, of course, the same age as us. Don Dunstan and both of my parents were all born within a year of each other, between September 1926 and May 1927, and he died two days after my mother's funeral.

But in terms of ideology and sensibility, Dunstan seemed like the same kind of person as those of my generation, except with power. Insofar as he felt like 'family', it wasn't because he was of our parents' generation, but because — unlike most of our parents — he seemed to believe the same things we believed about the way people should treat each other, about what the world ought to look like and how it ought to be run. Dunstan embodied the best of both worlds: he seemed a confident, reliable adult who knew exactly what he was doing, which is what everyone wants in a parent, but at the same time seemed also an exciting and energetic agent of change and liberation, the opposite of what any teenager or young adult expects a parent to be.

When I moved with my family from the country to the city at the beginning of 1966, the year I started high school, Dunstan was the State Attorney-General and Minister of Community Welfare and Aboriginal Affairs, under the ALP leadership of Premier Frank Walsh. At 39, with years of legal, political and parliamentary experience already behind him, Dunstan was the only member of Cabinet under 50. Spooked by the massive swing against Labor in the 1966 federal election, by the increasing influence of television — a medium of which the elderly Walsh was shy and nervous — and by the elevation of the young Steele Hall to the leadership of the LCL, the South Australian ALP decided in 1967 to replace Premier Frank Walsh, by then almost 70, with Dunstan, who slid uneventfully into the premiership. After a couple of years of instability — another two close elections within three years, a hung Parliament, and a major corrective shift in electoral boundaries — Dunstan regained office in 1970, when I was in my final year at school.

By the time he was forced — by strain, scandal and ill-health — to resign in February 1979, I was in my last year as a postgraduate student and about to head east in quest of a career; my first stretch as an Adelaidean had coincided almost exactly with Dunstan's time in power. And in one way, perhaps that period has been a bad thing for those who grew up with it as a norm and came to political consciousness while it was happening. For some of us, it set our lifelong expectations of political leadership far too high.

Reading *Felicia* 30 years after it was written and being reminded of how focused Dunstan was on the media, how clear his understanding was of media relations and how aware he was of the importance of television in particular, it begins to look as though the 1970s marked a turning point in the symbiotic relationship between politicians and journalists not only in South Australia but across Australia, and perhaps beyond. The Dunstan Decade coincided with the historical moment at which it was possible for public figures to maximise their use of the media, especially the relatively new medium of television, but still to use those things to achieve real policy ends, in contrast to the many contemporary politicians for whom image management and the gaming of the media cycle are no longer seen as means to an end but rather as ends in themselves.

For Dunstan, the Adelaide press, radio and TV stations were there to be wooed and used, to get the message out and charm the populace, and with the help and advice of his executive assistant, Peter Ward, he put a lot of thought, effort and imagination into what the best ways to go about this might be. His friend and federal Labor colleague Dr Neal Blewett called him 'a man for all media'. He had an early and sophisticated understanding of the media cycle and he timed announcements and events accordingly. He humiliated Opposition Leader Steele Hall, who had refused to debate him on television, by appearing on his own and gesturing towards the empty chair he had set up, unnecessarily pointing out that Hall was not sitting in it. He set up a monitoring service to record radio and TV broadcasts that might be pertinent to the government, which sounds both obvious and primitive now, but which at the time brought howls of protest from journalists and broadcasters, including – in a foreshadowing of things to come – Stewart Cockburn, *Advertiser* senior journalist and former press secretary to Robert Menzies, who protested about 'Big Brother'. The objectors called it 'surveillance' and demanded to know how a man so devoted to the cause of civil liberties could be prepared to do such a thing.

Dunstan had already spent decades building his political career on the power of his own physical presence in the city, doorknocking in his electorate, working on his appearance, polishing his vocal and performance skills, and playing a more and more prominent role as the Labor Party's attack dog in Parliament. He capitalised on all these things when he became Premier, and for several years they stood him in good stead: the tailor-made clothes, the carefully maintained body and the expensively trained voice looked and sounded good on radio and TV and in the press, and he used them all as vehicles to take people with him in his progressive and sometimes visionary advances and reforms. But as the decade wore on, it became clear that trouble could and would come from that direction too. For those who remember him with admiration and affection, there's always a temptation to idealise Dunstan and represent him as universally loved, which of course was very far from the case.

After several years as Dunstan's executive assistant, Ward had left the Premier's Department, taking over the Adelaide desk of *The Australian* and resuming his career as a journalist. In 1977 he began an investigation into whether the Special Branch of the SA Police was keeping secret files on 'more than 10,000 people not convicted of any offence in S.A.', sending a list of ten questions on this subject to the Premier. The list included a question asking whether Dunstan, long known as a civil libertarian, had known about it and had yet done nothing. There was enough in this story for it to blow up into a spectacular crisis for everyone involved: for the government, for the police, for Ward, who had not foreseen some of the possible consequences, and for the people who had reason to believe that if there were indeed a stash of secret dossiers, their own might be among them. On 17 January 1978, Police Commissioner Harold Salisbury was dismissed on the grounds that he had misled the government about the existence of the Special Branch secret files. Cockburn was among the many people on all sides of politics who were perturbed by this; he wrote about it in *The Advertiser* at length, and began collecting material for a book.

What lay behind the strange affair of the sacked Commissioner was a tangle of facts, implications, rivalries, political conflicts and tensions between individuals, friends, enemies, the Government, the Opposition, the judiciary and the police force, all going back to the 1950s, plus a dash of Cold War paranoia and another of leftover British imperialism. Salisbury, an Englishman born during World War I and imported from Britain for the job, seems from the statements he made at the time to have been preoccupied with the Profumo affair in particular and with Communism in general.

But the minotaur at the heart of this narrative labyrinth is the police attitude and response at the time to citizens in private or – especially – public life who were known or thought to be homosexual. A murky episode in the late 1960s in which Salisbury's conservative predecessor, Brigadier John McKinna, successfully undermined the career and reputation of Justice (and later Chief Justice) John Bray had been followed in 1972 by the shocking death of Adelaide University law lecturer Dr George Duncan, one of two men violently thrown into the River Torrens one night by two or more people whose identities have never been confirmed. The other victim, Roger James, who was young and fit, managed to get out of the river despite the fact that one of his legs had been broken, but Duncan, a frail man who couldn't swim, drowned. These events took place late one night at the well-known gay beat on the south bank of the Torrens and rumours began to circulate almost immediately that the police were involved. There have been three inquiries into Duncan's death; in 1988, two former Adelaide vice squad officers were charged with his manslaughter and acquitted, and an inquiry in 1990 concluded that there was 'insufficient evidence to charge any other person'.

By 1978, male homosexuality had been legal in South Australia for six years, but it was still stigmatised, and the police force argued that homosexuals in public life were peculiarly susceptible to blackmail and therefore needed to be under police surveillance as a matter of state security. There were rumours of 'pink files' being kept on those known to be, or suspected of being, homosexual.

One thing that emerges from a reading of various accounts of the Salisbury affair is the degree of antipathy and antagonism that seemed to exist between the police force and Dunstan's government, and some of the reasons for it. Dunstan had made a name for himself as a champion of civil liberties while Labor was still in Opposition, and there had been several cases in which allegations of police corruption and brutality had been brought to Dunstan's attention and taken by him to Playford, whose exaggerated respect for the institutions of authority – the police force, the courts, the Crown – ensured that they then sank like a stone. As early as 1963, writes Cockburn, after several incidents where private citizens had complained of police abusing their powers and authority and Dunstan had acted in their legal defence, citizens who felt themselves harassed by the police would reply 'I'll get Don Dunstan on to you.'

Cockburn's book, *The Salisbury Affair*, came out in 1979; though frankly partisan and quite damning in its implications for Dunstan, it remains the work of an intelligent and fair-minded journalist. But the other book about Dunstan that came out the same year was both less scrupulous and less justified. Dunstan had clashed repeatedly with 5DN radio journalist Mike McEwen and his news editor Des Ryan, and when their book *It's Grossly Improper* was published in 1979 it had about it a strong whiff of payback. It focuses on the details of Dunstan's relationship in the early 1970s with a man called John Ceruto, whom Ward has described as 'unattractively sycophantic and camp' and 'very, very strange', and who horrified Gough Whitlam when they met in Dunstan's company (though apparently Whitlam and Dunstan couldn't stand each other either).

By the time he was approached by Ryan and McEwen, Ceruto was a drug addict – he eventually died of an overdose in 1991 – and was persuaded by them to reminisce about his relationship with

Dunstan and to hand over, for money, a number of letters from him, some of which are unequivocally intimate and make Dunstan's lofty dismissal of the book as 'an absurd farrago of lies [and] crazed inventions' sound very hollow. The book's attempts to suggest some sort of sinister connection between Dunstan and Sydney underworld figure Abe Saffron, on the other hand, are limp and unconvincing. 'This insubstantial allegation of something not quite specific is the very stuff of the rumour machine in Adelaide,' Dunstan had written earlier, 'and enough for those involved in it to feed and delight on.'

But in any case, by the time *It's Grossly Improper* and *The Salisbury Affair* were published, Dunstan was already gone. His government had been damaged by the Salisbury sacking and its aftermath, and there had been widespread disquiet even among his supporters, since he appeared to be both on the attack and on the defensive, both demanding answers and covering up. The complexity of the story had something to do with this, but it was a bad look and his popularity took a beating. At the public meeting in mid-February at which Dunstan announced that there would be a Royal Commission into the sacking, I was one of the many people there who were admirers and supporters but had become profoundly anxious about the way the affair had been and was continuing to be handled. The meeting wasn't handled very well either: moments before Dr Neal Blewett got up to give his prepared speech about the lack of necessity for a Royal Commission, Dunstan said that he had changed his mind and would be announcing one after all. Cockburn, in his description of this meeting, which occurred at 10am on a hot day in February, sees fit to comment snidely and at surprising length on the fact that the Premier was informally dressed.

A couple of months later, the week after Easter 1978, Dunstan's second wife, Adele Koh, who was only 35, was found to be suffering from terminal cancer. Justice Roma Mitchell's report on the Royal Commission into the dismissal of Harold Salisbury was submitted to the Governor in May; in October, Adele Koh died. The combination of his wife's illness and death with the strain of the Salisbury affair and concern over the imminent publication of *It's Grossly Improper*, all while fulfilling his duties as Premier, was too much for Dunstan's own health; on 15 February 1979, a couple of days after he collapsed on the floor of Parliament and was ambulanced to hospital, he resigned from his position and retired from politics.

Another Adelaide journalist whose relationship with him had become increasingly scratchy during the 'Dunstan decade' was poet, editor and columnist Max Harris, the 'Angry Penguin' who had been the subject of the Ern Malley hoax in 1944. Generations of Adelaideans have cause to be grateful to Harris for his partnership with Mary Martin in establishing and maintaining the Mary Martin Bookshop. For my generation of friends and peers, living a student life, restless and isolated in a city that often felt too small and always felt too far away from the rest of the world, Mary Martin's was one of the focal points of the city. During the Dunstan years it was the best bookshop in town, one of Adelaide's few real gateways to the great world: it was the place you went to buy not only your Penguin paperback poets, with their mysterious voices from Spain and Poland and Czechoslovakia, but also your woven Greek shoulder bag to put them in.

Harris was five years older than Dunstan and a fellow Old Boy of St Peter's College. He had, like Dunstan, scooped the Saints pool of academic prizes in his day, but unlike Dunstan, he had saved himself from the bullying habitually visited on studious boys by exercising his skills on the football field. Harris and Dunstan had a bad start. In 1944, when Dunstan was a law/arts student at the University of Adelaide, he was still a political and cultural conservative; at the age of 18 he started a literary magazine of his own, *Grist*, in which he ridiculed Harris's Angry Penguins and the surrealist modernism that characterised their work.

Harris was later a columnist for *The Australian* and Adelaide's *Sunday Mail* for many years, including through much of Dunstan's tenure as Premier, and the relationship continued to deteriorate. Harris habitually referred to the Premier in his columns as 'Don baby (glitter, glitter)', an interesting bit of rhetorical shorthand implying that Dunstan's appeal was superficial and that his style concealed a less appealing substance. 'It was childish stuff,' says Dunstan, 'but it helped to create an atmosphere in which the actual achievements of Government were difficult to publicise.'

When Harris died early in 1995, a memorial service was held for him in Adelaide University's Bonython Hall, in which generations of students had donned cap and gown and stepped up to receive our degrees, and the slight tilt of whose floor was rumoured to be a deliberate feature ordered by the Bonython family, the pious Methodists who paid for the building of the hall, in order to discourage dancing. I was on my annual summer pilgrimage to Adelaide from Melbourne, and it was a hot day with a hard blue sky and a mica glitter bouncing off the parked cars and the pavements and plate-glass windows of North Terrace. Arriving at the entrance to the hall, I ran into the Adelaide novelist and poet Peter Goldsworthy and his first wife Helen — we are not related, as far as we can ascertain, but we are old friends — and the three of us went inside and sat down near the back.

The hall was almost full, and as we settled into our seats, some stirrings onstage quieted the crowd down to a murmur. Someone stepped up to the microphone, but before he could speak, there was a disturbance behind us at the door. Most people were too polite to turn around and look, but we heard the doors close, and then down the aisle came a small, fragile figure, walking slowly, his back and shoulders very straight. Not having turned to stare, we could see him only from behind as he passed us and proceeded slowly to the front of the hall, as though sure there would be a seat for him there. He wore a perfectly fitting stone-coloured linen safari suit, the quality beautiful, the style 20 years out of date but wholly appropriate for the weather, and those few who didn't recognise him by his clothes recognised him by his hair, now uniformly silver but if anything even more luxuriant than it had been in his youth, and unfashionably long. He was on his own.

Head high, unsmiling, Dunstan proceeded to the front and disappeared from sight. The entire hall, including the person at the microphone, discovered that we had been holding our collective breath, and let it out. Peter leaned over to whisper. 'Still knows how to make an entrance,' he said.

The pink shorts are a memorable garment in themselves, but they must be far more than that to have stuck so firmly in cultural memory for so long. They are a form of shorthand for the broad range of Dunstan-related things that they signify, and while the most obvious of these is Dunstan's own complex sexuality, there are several others: the reforms in matters of sexual freedom, including women's rights and the decriminalisation of homosexuality; the brightening-up of what had been a grey and genteel cultural backwater; the comfort and common sense of wearing clothes that suited the climate; and the shaking-up of conservative and code-bound institutions, not the least of which was Parliament itself.

'In matters of sexuality he was always ambiguously himself,' said Justice Michael Kirby at the NSW launch of the Don Dunstan Foundation in 1999. Dunstan spent the last 13 years of his life living quietly in his Norwood house with his partner Steven Cheng. Cheng was not the only male lover he had had, but he had also married twice and was the father of three children. Ward, who knew Dunstan well and who was himself living quietly but openly with a male partner – which was, as he points out, 'a defiant statement' while homosexuality was still illegal – said that he had not known for a long time what Dunstan's sexuality was, but had eventually concluded that he was bisexual. He was not, as many now mistakenly think he was, either openly, exclusively or unambiguously gay; he seems rather to have been one of those people for whom sexuality is less a matter of fixed identity than it is of mutable practice, something that more conservative Adelaideans found (and still do find) incomprehensible.

The idea that everything about him was somehow sexually irregular and perhaps sinister was extended in the vicious gossip that swirled around in conservative circles about his origins, much like the nonsense that US conservatives now spout about President Obama, and no doubt for the same reasons. Dunstan's dark colouring and the fact that he had been born in Fiji seem to have been the basis for the name-calling from conservatives who felt that he was a class traitor and who maintained that he was a 'Melanesian half-caste orphan bastard', though gossip was silent on how he could possibly have been both of these things at the same time.

One of these rumours went so far as to name names. But Cockburn's researches into his birth certificate and his parents' marriage certificate, and a photo of the young Dunstan with his father in Fiji, looking unmistakably like him, indicate how very unlikely this all is. Dunstan himself had an enlightening and enlightened take on it: 'The point was,' he wrote in 1978, 'that they thought it was something which would *discredit* me. Nowadays people would say "So what?"' He could also have pointed out that that darling of Adelaide's Old Families, Colonel William Light, was the illegitimate son of an illegitimate father and a Eurasian mother, brought up by relatives in England; if Dunstan had indeed been a Melanesian half-caste orphan bastard, he would simply have been continuing a rich old Adelaide tradition. Asked point-blank about these rumours at a press conference in 1970, he replied 'I am not half-caste, I am not Melanesian and I am not, in the technical sense, a bastard.'

The pink shorts also need to be seen in the context of cultural and social history. There had been a dramatic revolution during the late 1960s and early 1970s in the way people dressed, with a general loosening-up of standards and codes that was liberating for both sexes, especially in Adelaide, where dress codes had been rigid for a very long time; I have a vivid memory of my petite 40-ish mother ceremonially throwing away a hated girdle in about 1967 after pantyhose had been invented, up to which point girdles had been mandatory for 'decent' women whether they needed them or not. The interrelated meanings of sexuality, clothes and colour had recently had a workout in the musical *Hair*, which premiered in Adelaide in 1969 and featured a very funny song called 'My Conviction' about the fact that in most species it's the male, not the female, who sports bright colouring and luxuriant plumage.

Reporting on the 1972 Adelaide Festival, one Sydney journalist wrote breathlessly of 'a Premier who appears in the evening in a see-through white lace shirt, bulging over his pectorals, skin-tight black trousers, and ornate silver rings'. These, too, were the early years of glam rock: perhaps at least some of Dunstan's self-fashioning had its origins in Ziggy Stardust.

His commitment to keeping his private life private meant that Dunstan maintained a strange form of double-think on these matters, dismissing the rich symbolism of colour in a somewhat pompous bit of literal-mindedness as he concludes his discussion of the pink shorts in *Felicia*: 'The Premier's wearing *pink* was exploited as something carrying connotations of a public endorsement of effeminacy ... The use of colours in this way as carrying some sexual connotation is of course quite irrational and absurd.' This comes at the end of a discussion in which, for the best part of a page, he has been nattering on knowledgeably about fabric, cut and colour in a manner bordering on camp, and has invoked approvingly the views of William Morris, who in fact would have been horrified by the idea that colour could not legitimately be endowed with meaning.

But the pink shorts have connotations other than those related to Dunstan's own sexual orientation. Much of the social reform that his government achieved took place around matters to do with gender and sexuality, and as a garment that drew attention to both, it serves as a sort of *aide-memoire*. Dunstan took great pleasure in putting a bomb under stuffiness and regarded that trait as part of his persona; he would have enjoyed shocking the more staid elements of the populace, to say nothing of his fellow parliamentarians. And he was in his own decorative way a sort of one-man Rational Dress Society; having been born and brought up in Fiji meant that his earliest memories were of bright colours, informality and heat, and in dress as in other things he was a firm believer in living your life to fit the place in which you found yourself. His abolition of the dress rule in the Parliamentary Assembly (which had made it possible for him to turn up there wearing shorts in the first place) was part of his larger push to get South Australians living in harmony with their environment, and that included the heat.

More than anything else, though, the pink shorts are a reminder of Dunstan's own dynamic and sometimes dramatic physical presence, something no photograph or even footage can satisfactorily capture. At the height of his powers he was a man so full of intellectual energy that his physical presence around the city seemed luminous with it, and he dressed in a way that played that up, in colours and fabrics that shimmered and glowed. A former Dunstan aide, remembering what she calls his 'blue Nehru suit', puts her finger on the reason why his clothes always seemed so central a part of his persona: '. . . that particular fabric was a sort of a shot – I can't remember what it was, whether it was silk or a shot cotton of some sort, but it was a fabric that was full of light.'

9

The Frog Cake

The Balfours frog cake features prominently in any list of edibles that homesick Adelaideans miss. You can find these people huddled together in back-packer hostels or hotel foyers, at tourist attractions, in chat rooms across cyberspace or in the tea-rooms and kitchens of the workplaces to which their ambition has led them in Melbourne, Canberra, Sydney and beyond, seeking each other out in order to chant a litany of lost treats to fellow exiles who will understand. 'Frog cakes,' they moan. 'FruChocs. Fritz. Woodies' lemonade. Farmer's Union iced coffee. Haigh's chocolates. Coopers ale. Bickford's lime cordial. Kitchener buns. Golden North honey ice cream.'

With, one hopes, the exception of the ale and perhaps the iced coffee, these are the remembered treats of childhood, and they are yearned for just as much for their associations with home as for their deliciousness or quality. Few rational adults, for example, are foolhardy enough to eat a whole frog cake at one sitting; they are made mainly of sugar, as are most of the other things on that list. It may be partly because of Adelaide's relative geographical isolation that its home-grown treats are remembered with such ferocious fondness, because it's only comparatively recently that one has been able to buy some of them elsewhere. It may be a form of brand loyalty, but the brand in question is 'Adelaide'.

A Balfours frog cake is a classic *petit four*: a small cube of Genoa sponge cake, sliced through the middle (horizontally) to insert a layer of apricot jam, topped with a generous blob of artificial cream, and then cloaked in a smooth layer of fondant, decorated with a knife-slash through the top of the cake to represent an open froggy mouth, and two little dobs of royal icing for eyes. The original frog cakes were green, in the delicate pastel tint that was the strict baker's rule for food colouring; now they also come in pink and gooey chocolate brown, all three colours the violent neon kind that is fashionable in contemporary cake decoration. They seem a lot bigger than they used to be. They have their own Wikipedia entry, complete with

photographed cross-section. Bakers and confec-
tioners in other Australian states have of course
imitated the frog cake, but Balfours registered both
the name and the shape of the cake as an official
trademark in 2001.

James Calder and his wife Margaret Calder (*née*
Balfour) arrived in Adelaide from Edinburgh in
1852; they were on their way to the goldfields, but
for some reason decided to stay in Adelaide, where
they established their own goldmine instead, in the
shape of one of the most successful and long-lived
companies Adelaide has ever seen. A young descen-
dant in the family business, Gordon Balfour, travelled to Europe in the early 1920s and, no doubt
inspired by the magical patisseries of Paris, came
home with the idea of the frog cake. They began
being sold in 1922, at a time when Adelaide was
a city of cafes and tea-rooms; at one point Balfours had three cafes in business across the city
simultaneously. My father remembers being taken
to Europe as a little boy in the 1930s and staying
in a Scottish village with his mother's family, with
trips into nearby Stirling always involving a visit to
one of its cafes; his parents kept up the habit after
returning home to the farm, so any trip to the city
would involve a visit to Balfour's cafe as an outing

and a treat. My father goes all starry-eyed remembering the dark wood panelling, the white starched linen, the moulded-plaster ceilings, the silver plate. It certainly seems to have been regarded as a classy establishment; a big society wedding reception there is breathlessly reported in the *Register* in 1929.

In February 2010, almost 90 years after the first frog cake was served to a Balfours patron, my free weekly local paper *The Portside Messenger* reported some unusual catering at a rally to support a financially struggling football team, the Port Adelaide Magpies. This is the state-league Australian Rules team from which the second of Adelaide's two teams in the national AFL competition, confusingly also known as Port Adelaide or Port Power, was originally developed. The Port Adelaide Magpies are Adelaide's oldest football team, established in 1870; their colours, like Collingwood's, are black and white. And like Collingwood they are hated by all the state's football fans who do not actually barrack for them, and for much the same reasons: they are a team with working-class roots from a working-class suburb, carrying a largely undeserved reputation for rough and ungentlemanly play (something many Adelaideans abhor; we prefer, on the whole, to fight with words), onto which all manner of insecurities, class-based contempt and fear of difference is projected from the direction of the prosperous eastern suburbs, reinforcing my own view that the whole AFL culture is a psychoanalyst's paradise.

And now this proud 140-year-old club was in trouble. 'South Australia's iconic green frog cake is being transformed today to help support the Port Magpies' survival campaign,' reported the *Messenger*. 'About 500 black and white iced frog cakes will be delivered to the Port Club this afternoon, to be handed out at a supporters' rally this afternoon.' Anna Bryant from Balfours explained their reasoning, saying that the company wanted to show its support for the beleaguered club. 'Frog cakes and the Port Magpies are two iconic brands, with the frog cakes heritage-listed and much-loved in South Australia, just as the Port Magpies are,' she said.

This was not the first time that Balfours frog cakes had made an appearance iced in football club colours. They have been known to come in the colours of both AFL teams: the navy, red and gold of the Adelaide Crows, and the teal, silver, black and white of the Port Adelaide Power. And it gets worse: *The Advertiser* reported in April 2009 that plans were being made to build a new football stadium 'paying homage to South Australian culinary favourite the frog cake. Plans ... show the stadium ... complete with a lime green, retractable roof. A set of black eyes were to be painted on one half of the roof, giving the impression that the frog stadium was smiling whenever its roof opened.' So successfully deadpan was the style in which this article was written that it took some readers quite a while to realise what day it was: April the first. In 2001 frog cakes had had another outing in the world of sport: as part of her successful pitch to bring the World Police and Fire Games to Adelaide in 2007, SA Minister for Tourism Joan Hall served an assortment of them to the judges.

Such is their power as an Adelaide icon, presumably as a reminder of a happy childhood, that frog cakes sometimes feature even at life's most solemn rituals. I once saw in Balfours' shopfront window a wedding cake composed entirely of white frog cakes arranged in tiers, and I have been to at least one Adelaide funeral where frog cakes in assorted colours were served afterwards at the wake. Columnist and ABC broadcaster Peter Goers once went so far as to solemnly propose that the perennial problem of what to do about Victoria Square could be solved by erecting a Big Frog Cake in it, presumably as some sort of tourist attraction. Goers is someone who tends to polarise local opinion, but I am a fan: partly because of his progressive politics, partly because of the time he was speaking on the phone with some dedicated country listener to his ABC radio evening program and persuaded her to put the phone on top of her piano and play it — very well, as I recall — for his listeners, and partly because of an interview I once heard him conduct with a lively small boy at the Royal Adelaide Show, who was listing all the sugary, fatty things he'd had to eat that day, and all the rides he'd been on: 'And are you going to be sick now,' inquired Goers, 'or will you wait until you're back in the car?'

Balfours was not the only long-lived bakery and confectionery business established by 19th century settlers. Another of the treats that turns up on the list of homesick exiles, Menz FruChocs — little balls of dried apricot and peach coated in chocolate — also have their origins in Victorian Adelaide, with the Menz family arriving from Germany in 1849 and setting up a Wakefield Street bakery that was to become as successful and almost as long-lived an independent company as Balfours, though both have now been taken over by larger international firms. The biscuit manufacturing arm of the company was sold to Arnott's in 1962, which is why only South Australians know that Yo Yo Biscuits were originally made in Adelaide by Menz.

Nor was Balfours the only food business to import good ideas from Europe; the Adelaide chocolatier John Haigh, deciding at 19 that he would go into the family confectionery business, travelled to Switzerland in 1950 to be trained by Lindt & Sprüngli, where he learned what machinery to use and where to source the best ingredients. Part of the Haigh success story is the shrewd operation of the business over several generations of the family, including expansion to outlets in Melbourne and Sydney, but mostly it's just about the beautiful chocolate. Any excursion to their Visitors' Centre on Greenhill Road in the short week before Easter is something of a challenge; you shuffle around the large shopping area shoulder to shoulder with hundreds of other Adelaideans toting the shop's wire baskets, all milling about in different directions trying to grab the last chocolate Easter Bilby, Murray Cod or chicken-with-eggs before someone else gets to it, striking up lively conversations with total strangers about the pros and cons of violet creams, or whether peppermint goes better with milk chocolate or dark. Haigh's oldest Adelaide store is on the northeastern corner of the Rundle Mall intersection with King William Street, which is known as the Beehive Corner; this 19th century building was always called The Bee Hive but now it also sports, as decoration, a stylised beehive on which perches a gilded bee. It used to be a favourite meeting-place in the city. 'I'll meet you on the Beehive Corner' was the Adelaide equivalent of arrangements to meet at Sydney's Town Hall steps, or under the clock at Melbourne's Flinders Street Station.

'Food means cake and steak,' Patrick White complained, in the litany of damning observations about Australian culture and society in the late 1950s that formed much of his essay 'The Prodigal Son'. That was the essay in which he wrote about his decision to come home to Australia after the end of World War II and about his misgivings when he got here. In Adelaide as elsewhere, food did indeed still mean cake and steak in the 1950s, but what's often forgotten since Australia became a nation of foodies is that cake and steak are in themselves rather nice food, when well cooked, and there was plenty to be said for the good cooks of the period. But there's no denying that when you open a copy of an old South Australian recipe book – the *Green and Gold Cookbook* (1923), say, or a collection of old Country Women's Association recipes pre-1960 or so – you will be shocked by the amount of white sugar and white flour in the recipes, and startled by the absence of such Mediterranean notions as garlic or olive oil. Australian food, by and large, was British food, and the growing postwar influence on the latter of Elizabeth David was taking its time to cross the world.

But the wave of postwar European immigrants coming to Australia changed things in Adelaide as elsewhere; those who came to Adelaide were mainly Italian and Greek, and the influence of both communities was starting to be seen in Adelaide life by about the middle of the 1960s. By then you could get proper gelato and good espresso at Flash in Hindley Street, and real Italian pizza at Marcellina's or Don Giovanni's. And by the early 1970s there was a choice of two Greek restaurants, Hindley Street's Grecian Barbecue and The Iliad in Whitmore Square, where I washed dishes for a few weeks at the end of 1976. Flashy men would bring their skinny girlfriends there to eat; the men wolfed down huge plates of spicy lamb while the ever-dieting girlfriends picked listlessly at fish or chicken, ate three mouthfuls and left the rest. The restaurant kitchen had two doors – one through to the restaurant, and one out to the back yard, left open on the hot summer nights – and plate after plate of delicious but barely touched food came back to the kitchen through one door, while through the other I would hear strange noises outside in the dark as homeless men from the nearby Salvation Army hostel rummaged through the bins in the back yard.

I had already been introduced to Greek food by my classmates at Adelaide Girls' High, who brought vast plates and trays of delectable homemade baklava, as well as *galatouboureko* and *kourabiethes* – the lush Greek version of vanilla slice, and the little crescent-shaped shortbread biscuits studded with cloves and dusted with icing sugar – to school whenever we had any kind of fundraiser or fete, and who once put together a laboriously typed, hand-stapled booklet of Greek recipes that sold out on the spot.

And of course there was Chinese food: the Silver Dragon Restaurant in Rundle Street was not only the place where my adventurous mother persuaded my father into the taste for Chinese food that he still retains today, but also the scene of several childhood lessons in how to conduct yourself when dining in public. I can still hear her fiercely whispering 'Behave!' when the fidgeting or bickering at the table among her three daughters rose above acceptable levels, though she scorned the maternal admonition common in those days – 'Remember you're out!' – which implied that it was perfectly all right to behave like a rabid chimpanzee at home.

Given how novel and exciting pizza, souvlaki, chow mein, gelato and freshly brewed coffee all seemed in 1967, it's hard to believe how quickly Adelaide was transformed into a city of imaginative chefs, excellent restaurants offering a wide range of cuisines, Asian supermarkets and all manner of specialist food shops and stalls at the Central Market. It was serendipitous that a passionate foodie should have become Premier at exactly the time when people were beginning to embrace diversity in food (if in little else). This was, ironically, despite the fact that South Australia has had a quite ethnically diverse population since its earliest days. As students in the mid-1970s we were living on very little, but we would go without and save our earnings from waitressing or bartending or dishwashing for the occasional eating-out treat, and the favourite place for that was a little restaurant called Neddy's, tucked away in a run-down building in Hutt Street. The people who cooked for us there, just starting out in their subsequently extraordinary careers, were the young Philip Searle and the young Cheong Liew, who recalls that 'Adelaide was a most exciting city in the 1970s. Don Dunstan was in power and that actually had a big influence in my life, as he was a person who really gave ethnic groups an opportunity to do what they wanted to.' The Neddy's menu drew on his previous experiences as a cook, in Chinese, Greek and Spanish restaurants, as well as his own Malaysian heritage. It was all a very long way from a little green Paris-inspired novelty cake suitable for the tea-shops of the 1920s.

Dunstan, meanwhile, wrote and published a cookbook while Premier and opened a restaurant in his 60s, after he had retired from public life; one Adelaide historian, Peter Strawhan, completed an intriguing PhD thesis in 2004 entitled 'The importance of food and drink in the political and private life of Don Dunstan', a topic on which there exists more than enough material for such a thesis. For drink, too, abruptly became a hot

Adelaide topic in the 1970s, influenced to a large extent by the reforms to hotel and restaurant hours Dunstan brought in. While the Barossa Valley and McLaren Vale had been established wine regions for many years, the drinking of wine itself did not become popular or fashionable until about 1970, before which time 'real Australians' drank either beer or spirits. But winemakers like Peter Lehmann and Wolf Blass helped transform the South Australian wine industry into what we now know it to be. The ferocious Thistle Anderson had long ago vented her spleen on the wines of Adelaide, as well as everything else about the city:

> May a merciful God forgive Adelaide her wine, if he cannot find it in His heart to forgive the poor fools who drink it! ... had Omar lived in Adelaide, he would never have sung the praises of the vine at all, his glorious 'Rubaiyat' would never have been written, and the world would be the poorer for the loss.

Even allowing for the fact that she wrote *Arcadian Adelaide* in 1905, this now seems hilarious, but it is probably fairly accurate, and a very long way from the statistic offered to author Susan Mitchell by South Australia's then Minister for Tourism and former Mayor of Adelaide, Jane Lomax-Smith, in 2003: 'When I talk to people from overseas I always say "Seven per cent of the population, 70 per cent of the fine wine, it can't be bad." It's a great statistic.'

Meanwhile, in the Barossa Valley wine region, a woman called Maggie Beer and her husband Colin were working towards setting up their Pheasant Farm Restaurant, which opened in 1978 and specialised in locally raised game birds. Beer, like Liew and Searle, has since become one of Australia's best-known and influential cooks (she calls herself a cook rather than a chef), these days running a business selling her own specialist gourmet products, writing, giving demonstrations and running workshops, and appearing on TV in more than one of the vast number of cooking shows now filling our screens. The introduction on the home page of her Maggie's Farm Shop website encapsulates what has always seemed to me the best of Adelaide's food culture: a kind of in-placeness that starts with the ingredients rather than with the recipe, with whatever gift the place has chosen to bestow on that particular day. 'Whether a ute full of peaches or a trailer of blood oranges,' the introduction says, 'the produce always drives the product.'

On the other side of town, down in the McLaren Vale wine region to the south, this sense of connection between the cuisine and the locality becomes even stronger. Any Adelaidean seriously interested in food and drink knows that the country road from McLaren Vale to Willunga is a magical stretch, and not only because of the Tuscan-looking landscape of enamelled blue sky, gentle slopes planted with rows of vines, and picturesque hills in the distance. As you drive out of McLaren Vale you pass on your left an old farmhouse that you'd never know was a restaurant, for you need to know how to find the Salopian Inn before you go there. But if you go past it and keep heading south towards Willunga, there's a turnoff to the right just before you reach the town; the road lures you down an avenue of delicate, shivery, green-gold trees like something out of Rivendell, and delivers you at the door of Fox Creek Winery, where there really is a creek, and foxes, and they make beautiful crisp whites and a glamorous sparkling red called Vixen and a modest table red called Shadow's Run in memory of Shadow, their late Border Collie, who in his prime loved to run up and down the rows of vines whenever anybody twanged the wire of the supporting fence. The first time I heard the word 'locavore' I thought of that country road, and of a revelation I once had, looking out the window of the Salo-pian Inn at almond trees, olive trees and vines while we drank our wine and ate our warm bread with olive oil and dukkah: at least half of what we were eating and drinking could easily have come from the plants I was seeing out of the window.

Even allowing for the proliferation of farmers' markets over the last 10 years or so, including the large one in inner-suburban Wayville, the Adelaide Central Market is still the main market-shopping choice for many urban Adelaideans – especially when shopping for special occasions, holidays and feasts. Anyone foolhardy enough to go there on Christmas Eve risks being crushed to death, or at the very least rammed in the overfilled car park by someone suffering the combined effects of road rage and seasonal stress. The Central Market was established by the Adelaide City Council in 1869 and enjoys the same sort of strong and wide-spread public support as the Parklands, resisting all attempts to encroach on and 'develop' it. It has indeed been developed, but only enlarged, rather than internally changed, over the years.

For many Adelaideans its significance goes well beyond its function as a food market, too. Susan

Mitchell recalls its place in the rituals of her childhood:

> ... every Friday night my parents, Mitch and Jean, would take me to this market. While they were buying their fresh fruit and vegetables they would often leave me with the Salvation Army Band, which was always belting out rousing Christian tunes in the street in front of the entrance. I was given a tambourine so I could join in and I hit that tambourine like one possessed ... When my parents returned to pick me up, my cheeks flushed with tambourine passion, they always had a big bag of freshly roasted peanuts ... They smelled of innocence.

In the very early stages of writing this book I made use of various internet sites to ask Adelaide people for their memories of the Central Market. I thought of this charming story in Mitchell's book when one woman said that she had had a frightful childhood, abusive and violent, and she had always loved the market because it was the only place, all through her childhood, where she had ever felt safe. The Central Market, like the frog cake, is about a great deal more than just food.

10
The Concert Ticket

One day in November 2008 I spent a great deal of money on a small white piece of cardboard. 'Leconfield Winery', said this piece of cardboard, and 'BASS', and 'January 26, 2009', and – this was the important bit – 'Leonard Cohen'.

I first encountered Leonard Cohen's songs in 1969, when I was 16 and he was 35, and had been learning, playing, singing and listening to them on and off ever since. Forty years later, he was to tour Australia, mainly at outdoor venues like the big wineries, which had pretty grounds and big stretches of open space where a good stage could easily be put up. Not only was he coming to Adelaide, but he was to perform in one of its most beautiful bits of hinterland, the McLaren Vale wine district that Peter Goldsworthy calls the south wing of Paradise.

For me and for many of the friends who also

bought tickets, it really wasn't a matter of how good or otherwise Cohen was likely to be. Surely in his mid-70s he couldn't possibly still be much good as a performer, could he? Does the voice not go, by then, and what about the hearing, and the knees? Even in our 50s we were already starting to feel damaged and diminished ourselves; how must *he* be holding up, 20 years further down the line? Wasn't he just going on the road again of necessity, after 15 years, because his manager had run away with all his money and he needed to make some more?

So going to hear him was not so much about expecting a good concert as about nostalgia and devotion: about seeing in the flesh an icon who had influenced our way of seeing and given us a great deal of pleasure when we were young, in a city that seemed to us very far away from the great world. We were far away not just from Cohen's own equally small but – as we thought – so much more interesting and romantic home city of Montreal, but also from the Europe whose history permeated his songs, and from the timeless, operatic archetypes with which he anchored their vision: gods, soldiers, angels and saints who inhabited worlds of blood and smoke where lovers endlessly met and parted, worlds full of words like 'honour', 'jealous', 'partisan', 'gypsy'; like 'gold', 'glass', 'blue', 'song', 'night', 'blood', 'wine'. Along with other things, his music had brought the world to us in Adelaide, and now he was coming himself.

By the time I was 16 the glamour of Adelaide in comparison with the country town of child-hood was starting to wear off. At school I learned about the world beyond Adelaide not so much from lessons as from my Greek friends, from the small assortment of sophisticated, war-damaged, war-exhausted European women who taught us German and French, from the people who ran the 'Continental Cakes' stall at the Central Market just down the street from school and with whom we were encouraged to converse in German, and from the movies we saw when we traipsed off on school excursions to the Capri Cinema. Its screen was another window opening onto the world beyond Adelaide. It introduced us to the times and places of *Romeo and Juliet*, *Lord of the Flies*, *Zorba the Greek* and *Oh! What a Lovely War* – Renaissance Italy, 1930s Greece, war-benighted Belgium and the tropical islands of the Pacific – and to their big ideas: about love, war, death, sex, anarchy and chaotic night.

Endless prowling around the music shops in the city after school had brought both Leonard Cohen and Joni Mitchell to my attention, and from them and artists like them – singer-songwriters who, astonishingly, could write the words *and* the music *and* sing *and* play, for this, back then, was unusual – I was learning things about how to be an adult in the world, how to think about music, how to sing. The idea of young Australians learning things about sophistication of feeling and verbal expression from two Canadians (and indeed a third, Neil Young: 'Blue, blue windows behind the stars, yellow moon on the rise' is a line that all Adelaideans understand) should have alerted me to the fact that my own country and city might have things to offer too, but in Adelaide in the 1960s – and, alas, beyond – we were far too deeply steeped in the notion that London was the centre of all things to be able to make connections like that.

My friend R and I, who had listened to Cohen's music together since we were 17, decided we would get good seats – actual chairs, rather than BYO picnic rugs or unwieldy folding chairs – near the front. If we were going at all, we decided, we were going in style. So we were close enough, when the day arrived, to see everything: the carefully planned and perfectly rehearsed collaboration of the 10 musicians on the stage; the master guitarist from Barcelona in his big red chair with his guitar held in classical position and everyone, including Cohen, deferring to him; the trio of angel voices singing their delicate, brooding harmonies; and Cohen himself, slight and spry and beautifully dressed, looking 30 years younger from a distance – although the big screens showed all 74 of the years on his face, especially as the night grew late.

Stories had started to come west across the border from Sydney and Melbourne about what this show was like. But none of the reports had done it justice, for it was breathtaking in its precision and passion, its absence of any flaw. The songs reminded us how good they were and churned us up as they had always done, and when interval came as the sun was going down and relief set in at last from the liquefying heat, the audience got up and stretched and milled around, dishevelled, summer-clad, silhouettes rimmed in gold as the sun set behind us and looking like a bigger and even more laid-back antipodean version of Renoir's 'The Luncheon of the Boating Party', all summer hats and singlets and glasses of wine. The crowd looked as though it had been put under some sort of spell; many people were so enchanted that they could barely speak. Then as the dusk deepened to dark blue and the moon rose and the stars came out, Cohen came back and began his second set by saying 'It's a privilege to play in this peaceful country', and some of us thought about that for a minute and began to cry.

Anyone else who grew up in Adelaide, Brisbane, Canberra, Darwin, Hobart or Perth, much less anywhere smaller, will have some idea of what all this might have meant. Of all Australian citizens, probably only those of Sydney and Melbourne can take it for granted that if some megastar or international exhibition or magnificent theatre production comes to Australia, they will be able to see them, money permitting, without actually having to get on a plane. For us, the rarity of the Cohen concert was a large part of what made it so important: much of its value lay precisely in the fact that it had never occurred to us that Cohen might go on tour again, or that, if he did, he'd come to Adelaide.

Still, the Adelaidean sense of being perennially left out or overlooked by the stars of the world had lessened somewhat after 1960, which was the year of the first Adelaide Festival of the Arts. The festival was largely the privilege and preserve of the moneyed classes for its first 10 years or so, but here, as in the rest of the First World, old money is not what it used to be; over the last few decades much has been done, by Dunstan and later by others, including Robyn Archer, to democratise and popularise both the practice and the patronage of the arts, long regarded as an essential part of Adelaide's identity.

The multi-talented Archer is one of Adelaide's most successful and impressive daughters: graduate of tough Enfield High in the northern suburbs; regular teenage performer on *The Country and Western Hour* on South Australian Saturday night television in the 1960s, produced at Channel Nine in Adelaide and a never-missed show in our house; star of a university revue skit from the early 1970s in which she played Eve, wearing her own waist-length red hair and a pair of green knickers presumably intended to signify a fig leaf, and carrying, for reasons now lost to me, a pizza; hired entertainer singing dirty songs at workplace outings in pubs (I know this because I once went to one, and learned several new words); frank and articulate feminist; and generally just not the Old Adelaide Families' cup of tea, despite her many achievements in music and theatre, her Honours degree in literature, her standing as an artist, intellectual and internationalist, and the formal honours conferred on her by the governments of several countries, including her own.

She was the first person Adelaide ever heard sing the songs of Brecht and Weill, and she graced a number of Adelaide Festivals as a performer, including one memorable concert in 1978, when, having sung songs from an album of poems by Australian women writers that she'd set to music and recorded, she moved on to a set of classic 1960s rock'n'roll, instructing the respectful Writers' Week audience to push all the chairs back to the wall and dance, which we did. She was Director of the 1998 and 2000 Adelaide Festivals and gave them a stronger focus on community and easy access than they had ever had before; the closing event of the 1998 Festival, created and directed by the legendary Australian chef and writer Gay Bilson, was called 'Loaves and Fishes' and involved a communal feeding of 2000 people in the open on the banks of the Torrens, including theatrical performances and music.

Every two years for the last half-century – and from 2012 the festival will be an annual event – Adelaide has transformed itself for three weeks in March into a place where every theatre and restaurant and car park is always full, where there are flags and banners and crowds in the streets and spectacular lights and more crowds at night. In the 1960s and 1970s, when Adelaide was still not at all used to being visited by the legends of entertainment and the arts, we were starry-eyed when Nureyev came, and Hephzibah Menuhin, and Peter Brook; Acker Bilk and Marlene Dietrich; Benjamin Britten and Peter Pears. Anthony Burgess, Ted Hughes, Nadine Gordimer were all guests in the early years of Writers' Week, and later J.M. Coetzee came and stayed; when asked about his reasons for moving to Australia, he replied 'I was attracted by the free and generous spirit of the people, by the beauty of the land itself, and – when I first saw Adelaide – by the grace of the city that I now have the honour of calling my home.'

Given what I have already written in this book, it's hard to believe that when we were young, so many of us thought Adelaide had nothing to give us; that being left off some touring star's itinerary, because the profits from a smaller population weren't big enough to cancel out the nuisance of adding an extra leg to the tour, was enough to make us feel that our city wasn't good enough for us either. I now think we were simply projecting, mistaking 'Adelaide' for what was in fact the sketchy thinness, so far, of our own young lives reflected back at us. Some of us were suffering, perhaps, from a version of the childhood fantasy that Freud calls the family romance: the child's fantasy that she is adopted, that her 'real' parents are better, richer, more famous, and more beautiful than these people calling themselves her mother and father, and that one day she will be reunited with her real parents and leave these ordinary hardworking plebs far behind.

In some such way did generations of young Australians (and perhaps of Adelaideans more than most) hanker for their imagined real mother: England. It must be a common postcolonial condition, an inherited hangover from being brought up in an outpost of empire – and colonial Adelaide always prided itself on being a proper English province, not just a colony, whatever they thought the distinction to be. Some Adelaideans have never really recovered from all this even now, and retain the niggling sense that they truly belong somewhere better, somewhere bigger or classier, with more theatres in it, more celebrities, better newspapers, more people to have sex with, funnier comedians, more shops open later at night.

I imagine most small-to-medium provincial cities in most countries have their share of these malcontents, but it's easy to feel there must be more to life when you're in a small, young city in a small, young country and therefore separated at two removes from the bright lights and the world stage. And many of us were also driven by ambition and curiosity about what we could achieve, how far we could go, and whether, if we moved to a bigger pond, we would swim or drown. 'Real life was elsewhere,' writes Paul Kelly of his restless 17-year-old Adelaide self. 'I couldn't get out of town fast enough. Of course, everything was happening in Adelaide all along, and still is ... enough for a thousand novels, movies, songs. I never had to leave home at all.' Barbara Hanrahan, who went to London at 23 and stayed there for some years, came to much the same conclusion: 'I began to write about my childhood ... If I wrote about my beginnings in that working-class suburb of Adelaide caringly enough, I might be writing about a place in a Greek myth.'

You have to go away and have adventures in order to come home enriched; quite apart from anything else, what knows she of Adelaide who only Adelaide knows? But as we listened to Leonard Cohen on that hot night in the Southern Vales, it occurred to me that he too, like Kelly and Hanrahan, could have found everything he needed for his art in his own family and home town of Montreal, given the assortment of loyalties and cultures into which he was born: a Polish-Lithuanian-Russian Jewish family in a Francophone city, bigger than Adelaide but smaller than Brisbane, in a country that was, like ours, a part of the British Commonwealth. Every defining characteristic of his songs – the European sensibility, the Old Testament imagery, the close attention to the sound of language, the sense of being an outsider – was all already there in his childhood, waiting to unfurl.

When Andrew Denton interviewed Antonio Banderas in 2004, he mentioned that Banderas spends a lot of time working in the United States but tries to get home to Málaga in Spain for part of every year, and then asked, 'What is it that you most crave about Spain, that you miss?' Banderas replied, 'Well, family, friends and the food. And the type of life, in a way. Málaga is a very human city ... It's 600,000 people, and you've got everything that you may need ... but you have the space for a comfortable, beautiful life.'

Ask any happy Adelaidean why she or he is happy and you will get a very similar reply, though the comfortableness of Adelaideans is what many people hold against us, seeing it as smugness and complacency. And there is certainly some of that, but often what is being read as complacency or torpor is actually just simple happiness. There is much to be said for a city built on a human scale, one in which you do not feel overwhelmed. As though continuing a conversation with his readers – and perhaps himself – that he began in 1985, in his essay about knowing a place 'from my body outwards', David Malouf published in March 2011 an essay on happiness in which he concludes that 'a man can be happy … if the world he is in, and has to deal with, still has what he feels to be "human" dimensions; is still proportionate to what his body can recognise and encompass … What is human is what we can keep track of. In terms of space this means what is within sight, what is local and close; within reach, within touch.' Twice the size of Málaga, Adelaide is if anything in danger of becoming too big for this particular form of comfort, but those of us who know it well still have some sense of being able to walk from one of its significant sites to the next without becoming bewildered or exhausted, pummelled by traffic, crowds and noise. Of course it does not have the ancient history or romance of that beautiful Andalusian city, but it does have its own considerable beauty.

And as I've come to see very clearly as I wrote this book, Adelaide is piling up history as fast as it can, built on the land of the displaced Kaurna and haunted by the dead. Robert Gouger watched his wife die here and then his son, and buried them in the place he had done so much to create. From his high pedestal on the hill, the statue of Colonel Light points across to his own burial place in the heart of the square that bears his name, while somewhere the Beaumont children too lie dead, undiscovered but always present in the city's mind. The small fragments of tooth and bone that were once Charles Cameron Kingston are now laid back to rest in his unquiet grave, having given up their secrets a century after his death. The memory of the small, dark, vivid presence that was Don Dunstan glitters and shines, in his garden, at his microphone, in union meetings and the foyers of theatres; and the uncanny statues of Dame Roma and Bradman and Captain Sturt seem eternally about to step down from their pedestals and go in search of Adelaide's courts and offices, its theatres and sports grounds, its parties and pubs and cabs and clubs, as they did in life.

And that's just the dead. The culture of any place is not so much about its size or sophistication as about the living body in the city: the working, singing, crying, swimming, eating, sleeping, reading body, the dancing body, the body making love or art, the body sick unto death, the body that so resembles those of family members who live here too, the body punished or beaten, the sun-warmed body, the body that your home-town friends remember from when it was young, the maternal body wheeling the sleeping baby in the pram through the cemetery past the marble names of the friendly dead, the body as it moves through a city's schools and hospitals and offices and shops, taking their shape, bearing their stamp, and goes home to sleep in a quiet street at the end of the day. To be a citizen of Adelaide is to know some of its streets and parks and houses from your body outwards, where life is measured not in time but in accretions of lived experience; where friendship is recorded not by duration but by the number of places on the map where there have been outbreaks of music or life-changing conversations about love and work; where the distance from your first kiss to the death of your mother is not three decades but a short, pretty walk: up through the park, across the bridge, and down the road that curves away from the river.

Acknowledgments

General Sources

The National Library of Australia's magnificent and enormous Australian Newspaper Digitisation Program may be the biggest single advance in scholarly resources in the history of Australian Studies. I could not have written this book without it.

The *Australian Dictionary of Biography Online* and the wonderfully readable and informative *Adelaide From Colony to Jubilee: A Sense of Difference* (Adelaide: Savvas Publishing, 1985) by Derek Whitelock have been invaluable resources for almost every chapter of this book.

1 Introduction: Contradictions

The story of Queen Adelaide's embroidered gown is told in the Adelaide printmaker and novelist Barbara Hanrahan's essay 'Weird Adelaide', which originally appeared in the March 1988 issue of *The*

Adelaide Review and was reprinted in Gillian Whit-lock's anthology *Eight Voices of the Eighties* (Brisbane: University of Queensland Press [UQP], 1989). While I could find no other written account of this, the President of the Queen Adelaide Society, Triss Roberts, confirms that it's true.

George Seddon discusses the extent to which 'Mediterranean' is a misnomer for the climates of Adelaide and Perth in 'Mediterraneity', Chapter 6 of his *The Old Country: Australian Landscapes, Plants and People* (Melbourne: Cambridge University Press (CUP), 2005), and again in more detail in 'Adelaide's Alter-Egos', published in *The Adelaide Park-lands Symposium – A Balancing Act: Past-Present-Future* (Adelaide: Centre for Settlement Studies and the Bob Hawke Prime Ministerial Centre, University of South Australia, 2006, pp. 185–97).

The Aboriginal people of the Adelaide Plains are known as the Kaurna. Anthropologist Steve Hemming traces 'the origin and meaning of the term Kaurna and the history of its use' in his article '"Kaurna" Identity: A Brief History', published in a special double issue of the *Journal of the Anthropological Society of South Australia*, December 1990, pp. 126–42.

The point about South Australia's 'real' birthday

is made by P.A. Howell in 'The South Australia Act, 1834', Chapter 2 of *The Flinders History of South Australia: Political History* (Kent Town SA: Wakefield Press, 1986, pp. 26–51).

'Systematic colonisation' was what Edward Gibbon Wakefield called his scheme for successful colonisation; it was based largely on the reasons he had seen previous colonies fail. The idea was that the British government would raise money by the controlled sale of land in the colonies to those who could afford to buy it, and use the money thus gained to pay for the emigration of young couples and families who would make up the labour force necessary to run households and farms, thereby maintaining a three-way balance among capital, labour and land, as well as avoiding the 'evils' a male-heavy population could lead to. The theory had a sort of clockwork logic and beauty that didn't always work out in practice.

The theory that it was actually George Kingston who should be given the credit for choosing the site and designing the layout of Adelaide was put forward by Donald Leslie Johnson and Donald Langmead in *The Adelaide City Plan: Fiction and Fact* (Kent Town SA: Wakefield Press, 1986).

David Malouf's essay 'A First Place: the Mapping of a World' was the 14th Herbert Blaiklock Memorial Lecture, delivered at the University of Sydney on 26 September 1984 and first published in *Southerly* 45 (1985), pp. 3–10.

2 The Map

Colonel Light's rationalisation for choosing the site of Adelaide is given in *A Brief Journal of the Proceedings of William Light, Late Surveyor-General of the Province of South Australia: with a few remarks on some of the objections that have been made to them* (Adelaide: Archibald Macdougall, 1839, p. 43).

The reason for Adelaide's east–west streets changing their names when they get to King William Street is given at the History South Australia website: http://www.historysouthaustralia.net/STlist4.htm#kw, accessed 20 February 2011.

Thistle Anderson's *Arcadian Adelaide* (Kent Town SA: Wakefield Press, 1985) was first published in 1905 and reprinted by the Wakefield Press with an essay by historian Derek Whitelock, 'Thistle Anderson in Edwardian Adelaide', in which he unearths some facts about the handsome young Thistle and the almost hysterically nasty little book – no less unpleasant for being on target so often in its criticism of the Adelaide citizenry's prudery, self-satisfaction and 'Churchianity' – which she claims was 'intended merely as a playful skit' and which Whitelock calls 'a thistle under the municipal bottom'.

The information about Sophie van Rood and The Banana Room is not only from my memories but also from RMIT University's website 'Cyberfibres,' at http://www.cyberfibres.rmit.edu.au/biogs/TRC0540b.htm, accessed 20 February 2011. The history of the Sym Choon family is told at the current business's website: http://www.missgladyssymchoon.com.au, accessed 17 February 2011.

A description of the use that painter Barbara Robertson made in her work of the view from her Grote Street studio, along with reproductions of some of the paintings, can be found in Lorraine McLoughlin's independently published *Barbara Robertson: An Australian Artist's Life* (2009).

Councillor Francis Wong is quoted in 'Surveillance boost for Gouger Street', ABC News online, 17 June 2008: http://www.abc.net.au/news/stories/2008/06/17/2276675.htm, accessed 7 February 2011.

Peter Morton's description of Victoria Square in 1878 appears in his *After Light: A History of the City of Adelaide and its Council, 1878–1928* (Kent Town SA: Wakefield Press, 1996, p. 20).

The report of the Adelaide City Council meeting on 2 April 2001 that voted for the 'dry zone' appeared in *Green Left Weekly* online, in John McGill and Bronwen Beechey's 'Adelaide council votes for dry zone', 11 April 2001, at http://www.greenleft.org.au/node/25285, accessed 18 February 2011. Terry Plane's article discussing the decision appeared in the Adelaide *City Messenger* on 4 April 2001 and is quoted in McGill and Beechey's article. Sister Janet Mead's steady opposition to the dry zone, still being maintained eight years on, is quoted in Daniel Wills's 'Booze ban raises racial issues', on the *Adelaide Advertiser*'s online site *AdelaideNow*, 2 October 2009: http://www.adelaidenow.com.au/news/booze-ban-raises-racial-issues/story-e6freo8c-1225782298166, accessed 18 February 2011. Juan Davila's excellent point about the perversity of a dry zone in a city that relies so heavily on its wine industry is quoted in Adelaide novelist Tracy Crisp's essay 'Destination: Adelaide', in *The Griffith REVIEW*, Edition 15: 'Divided Nation', at http://www.griffithreview.com/edition15/82-essay/165.html?start=1, accessed 18 February 2011.

Peter Goers' tongue-in-cheek suggestions for the improvement of Victoria Square are made in 'A Little Lunacy on Victoria Square', in *The Sunday Mail*, 18 August 2007, and on the *AdelaideNow* website, http://www.adelaidenow.com.au/news/opinion/a-little-lunacy-on-victoria-square/story-e6freafu-1111114214495, accessed 17 February 2011.

Uncle Lewis Yerloburka O'Brien's explanation and diagram of the kangaroo outlined by the streets of Adelaide appears in his memoir *And the Clock Struck Thirteen* (Kent Town SA: Wakefield Press, 2007, pp. 200–01). In her beautiful and scholarly book *Visions of Adelaide 1836–1886* (Adelaide: Art Gallery of South Australia, 2005, p. 120), curator Tracey Lock-Weir reports a conversation with O'Brien about this kangaroo: 'O'Brien believes Light absorbed the spiritual essence of the land when placing the streets and site of Adelaide.' O'Brien and others have also expressed this view elsewhere when speaking of the placement of Victoria Square/Tarndanyangga in the centre of the city's design.

Mark Twain's account of his trip down through the Adelaide Hills is from *Mark Twain in Australia and New Zealand*, quoted in Derek Whitelock's

Adelaide From Colony to Jubilee: A Sense of Difference (Adelaide: Savvas Publishing, 1985, p. 258), and Hal Porter's is in the second volume of his auto-biography, *The Paper Chase* (Brisbane: UQP, 1980, pp. 153–54). Peter Goldsworthy's description of a drive through the Hills on a sunny day when you're in love appears on the first page of his novel *Three Dog Night* (Melbourne: Viking, 2003), in which the Adelaide Hills almost have the status and presence of a main character.

3 The Painting

Unless otherwise stated, the information in this chapter about Charles Hill, including commentary on the Proclamation painting, is taken either from his obituary in *The Advertiser* (18 September 1915, p. 16), or from the file on Hill held by the Research Library of the Art Gallery of South Australia, many of the items in which are unsigned and one of which describes the condition of the painting as 'slightly grubby in parts'.

Material about Robert Gouger comes from his *South Australia in 1837: in a series of letters, with a postscript as to 1838* (London: Harvey & Darton, 1838), from *The Founding of South Australia: as recorded in the journals of Mr. Robert Gouger, first Colonial Sec-*

retary, edited with additional material by Edwin Hodder (London: Sampson Low, Marston and Company, 1898), from Douglas Pike's *Paradise of Dissent: South Australia 1829–1857* (London: Longmans, Green & Co., 1957), and from the *Australian Dictionary of Biography Online (ADB) Online* entry for Gouger: http://adbonline.anu.edu.au/biogs/A010423b. htm, accessed 8 February 2011.

Gouger's account of the original Proclamation ceremony, and of his feelings on the birth of his son the following day, appears in his 'Memoranda of a Residence in Holdfast Bay', quoted in Hodder, pp. 203–04.

The summary of Wakefield's ideas about 'systematic colonisation' and the sale of land to fund the emigration of couples to work as labourers and servants is taken from the *ADB Online* entry for him: http://www.adbonline.anu.edu.au/biogs/ A020510b.htm, accessed 8 February 2011.

The text of the Proclamation was published on the front page of the first issue of the Colony's first newspaper, *The South Australian Gazette and Colonial Register*, on 3 June 1836.

Gouger expresses his anxiety about the treatment of the Aborigines in Letter III of *South Australia in 1837*, on p. 46. The passage about Aboriginal rights to land from the 1836 Letters Patent is quoted in 'The South Australia Act, 1834' by P.A. Howell, in *The Flinders History of South Australia: Political History*, edited by Dean Jaensch (Kent Town SA: Wakefield Press, 1986, p. 41).

The tactful-sounding remark about Gouger's 'warm' temperament is made by the Rev. John Blacket in his history of South Australian colonisation, first published serially in 1903: 'Our Early History: The Romance of South Australian Colonisation 1836–1857', Chapter VII, appeared in *The Advertiser*, on 12 September 1903, p. 9. This is also the source of the exhortation to Adelaideans to remember Gouger when walking down 'Gouger-street', and be grateful. In his *Paradise of Dissent*, a book that over 50 years later is still regarded as the definitive history of South Australia's early years, Douglas Pike gives a detailed biography and character sketch of Gouger which includes the sad story of the illusory mountain range.

Margaret Stevenson's comments on the faces in the crowd on the first Proclamation Day are quoted in Geoffrey Dutton and David Elder's *Colonel William Light – Founder of a City* (Melbourne: Melbourne University Press [MUP], 1991, p. 184). They stand in strange contrast to the cheery observation of her fellow-colonist Mrs Robert Thomas, who had arrived on an earlier ship and who wrote in her diary that the *Buffalo* passengers 'all seemed highly delighted with our village, as I may call it, consisting now of about forty tents and huts'. And so they might, after months at sea with Captain Hindmarsh and his smelly menagerie.

The information about Adelaide's earliest colonial artists comes from Tracey Lock-Weir's detailed, engaging and valuable Introduction to her *Visions of Adelaide, 1836–1886*.

Some of the material about the life and work of Charles Hill is taken from an article by R.G. Apple-yard in the *Bulletin of the National Gallery of South Australia* (January 1967). The information about Hill's role in the School of Design is from George E. Loyau's *Notable South Australians; Or, Colonists Past and Present* (Adelaide: George E. Loyau, 1935, p. 125).

An early sketch of Gouger's tent by the colonial artist John Skipper, an identified figure in Hill's painting, shows the arched gum tree at some distance from Gouger's tent and a tall, straight, shady one practically next to it; given the weather, it seems far more likely that the colonists would have gathered in shade, none of which was provided by the almost-bare arched tree. The 1868 photograph 'The Proclamation Tree' is reproduced in Julie Robinson's *A Century in Focus: South Australian Photography 1840s–1940s* (Adelaide: Art Gallery of South Australia, 2007, p. 81), as is the Duryea panorama, on pp. 73–75. Mark Twain is quoted in the same book, in the commentary on the notes on 'The Proclamation Tree' by Elspeth Pitt, p. 80.

Geoffrey Dutton's dismissal of the Proclamation as 'Hindmarsh's little circus' is consistent with the partisan tone of his near-hagiographic biography of Light, which is nonetheless elegant and lively, and many other sources seem to confirm that Light really was an extraordinarily gifted and likable person. A reproduction of the painting appeared in *The Adelaide Review* on 30 December 1998 with unsigned commentary observing that 'The painted has diplomatically placed Col. William Light (in centre of group in white breeches) next to Gov. Hindmarsh. In reality, Col. Light was not present, wishing to be as far as possible from his major critic.' Whoever wrote this was probably using Dutton as a source; both are ignoring the fact that at that time the conflict between Light and Hindmarsh, who were old friends, had not yet developed, though Light was already beginning to feel hounded.

4 The Statue

As well as the general sources listed above, notably the *ADB Online* and the National Library of Australia's *Trove*, my two main sources of information about Colonel Light and his life and times for this chapter are Douglas Pike's *Paradise of Dissent* and the 1991 edition of Geoffrey Dutton's biography of Light. First published in its original form in 1960, Dutton and David Elder's *Colonel William Light: Founder of a City* (Melbourne: MUP, 1991) includes in this edition some extra material, answers some critics and challengers, and credits David Elder as co-author. The other – and even more – indispensable general source for this chapter is Simon Cameron's beautiful little book *Silent Witnesses: Adelaide's Statues and Monuments* (Kent Town SA: Wakefield Press, 1997), which includes information, photographs and stories about the statues of Adelaide.

Paul Kelly's song 'Adelaide' is track 7 on his first album *Post* (1985) and was re-released on his second, *Gossip* (1986). The lyrics are as written in his memoir *How to Make Gravy* (Melbourne: Hamish Hamilton, 2010, p. 10).

The inscription on the pedestal about Light's 'enemies' is taken from the Preface to Light's *A Brief Journal* (p. iv). This document tells us a lot about

Light, including the facility with language that he shared with a number of his fellow colonists, especially when he lost his temper: 'How stupid the Commissioners must have been in sending me out here without furnishing me with a magic wand to raise Elysiums for gentlemen so hard to please.' Light would have enjoyed J.M. Coetzee's comment about his thoughts on first seeing Adelaide: "What kind of place is this?" I asked myself. "Is this paradise on Earth? What does one have to do to live here? Does one have to die first?"

Light's frustrated assessment that he should have been sent at least six months before the colonists is quoted in Dutton and Elder, p. 179.

Johnson and Longmead's *The Adelaide City Plan: Fiction and Fact* details the authors' research into Kingston's part in the choice and surveying of the Adelaide city site.

The comment about the absence of 'horse, pony or ox' for transport is quoted in Dutton and Elder, p. 182.

The theory that Light had failed to gain employment in the East India Company because of his mixed racial origins is also expressed by the redoubtable Lady Jane Franklin, who with her husband Sir John spent some time in Australia – he was

Lieutenant-Governor of Van Diemen's Land from 1836 to 1843, the years preceding his ill-fated Arctic expedition. Lady Jane's diary is quoted in Dutton and Elder, p. 200: 'Mr Light's son [i.e. Mr Francis Light's son William] had wished to enter East India Company's service, but he was refused on being halfcaste – afterwards got into Reg. of the Line – on losing his fortune he applied for service to Pasha of Egypt and then came out here.'

The cinematic tale of Light's bold reconnaissance mission in Spain is told by Sir William Napier in his *History of the War in the Peninsula* (1828) and quoted in Dutton and Elder, p. 69. Light had a wide assortment of gifts that made him valuable in the field, notably his skill with languages and his talent for drawing and sketching the terrain.

The 'disgust and hatred' letter from Light to Colonel Torrens was written on 22 May 1838, and is reproduced with much other correspondence to and from Light in [Miss] M.P. Mayo's *The Life and Letters of Col. William Light* (Adelaide: F.W. Preece & Sons, 1937, p. 238). The speeches at the dinner in his honour two weeks later are quoted in Dutton and Elder, p. 254.

The remark about the circumstances of Light's death and his not being able to marry Maria or enjoy

Adelaide (or, presumably, Maria, given how ill he was by now) is made in Dutton and Elder, p. 275.

Manning Clark's *A History of Australia, Volume IV: The Earth Abideth Forever, 1851–1888* (Melbourne: MUP, 1978) tells of the Burke and Wills expedition in great detail, but of the several Stuart expeditions, including the successful one, barely at all. Brian Matthews, in *Manning Clark: A Life* (Sydney: Allen & Unwin, 2008, p. 338) says that Clark's sketch of John McDouall Stuart is done 'sympathetically', but here I think it's Matthews who is being overly sympathetic to Clark. Given Clark's own problems with alcohol, as described in Matthews's generous but clear-eyed biography, his portrait of Stuart is probably partly projection.

The *ADB Online* entry for Charles Cameron Kingston, where the tale of the duel is told, is at http://adbonline.anu.edu.au/biogs/A090 604b.htm, accessed 24 February 2011. The story of the proposed exhumation was reported online in *The Australian* on 27 May 2008, at http://www.theaustralian.com.au/news/womanising-politics-pioneer-exhumed/story-e6frg6p6-1111116452080, and the results were reported at *The Advertiser*'s website, *AdelaideNow*, on 12 May 2010, at http://www.adelaidenow.com.

au/dna-proves-charles-kingston-theory/story-e6frea6u-1225865242518, both accessed 27 February 2011. The latter is the article in which Malcolm Simpson is quoted.

The rather harsh assessment of Captain Charles Sturt as 'a born loser' in public life can be found in the entry on Sturt in the *ADB Online*, at http://adbonline.anu.edu.au/biogs/A020458b.htm, accessed 24 February 2011.

Information about the life of Dame Roma Mitchell is taken from Susan Magarey and Kerrie Round's lively biography *Roma the First* (Kent Town SA: Wakefield Press, 2007); the quip about being called 'Mr Justice' is quoted on p. 161.

The description of Robert Hannaford working on the statue of Sir Donald Bradman is from John Neyland's *Robert Hannaford: Natural Eye* (Kent Town SA: Wakefield Press, 2007, p. 27).

The story of the lipstick on the horses' noses and the beautiful description of a night-time Adelaide filled with light — they don't make journalists like they used to — come from an article in *The Advertiser* on Friday 17 August 1945, on p. 6, with the magnificent triple-barrelled heading 'UNPRECEDENTED CITY SCENES: Work Forgotten in Thrill of News: 300,000 People In

Streets', beginning 'Never has Adelaide witnessed such scenes as those of Wednesday, when the pent-up tension of six years of war, accentuated by premature announcements of peace, burst into an unrestrained expression of relief and thankfulness.' The description of the fireworks is from a different article, also on p. 6, of the same edition: 'FIREWORKS LAST NIGHT: Seething Mass in Adelaide'.

Keith Phillips' 'Pyrotechny' is reproduced and discussed in Julie Robinson's *A Century in Focus: South Australian Photography 1840s–1940s* and appears in its cover design.

The Venerable Bede's image of the swallow (in some versions a sparrow) in the dining-hall is used by A. Grenfell Price to describe Light's Adelaide sojourn in *Founders and Pioneers of South Australia* (Adelaide: F.W. Preece and Sons, 1929) and quoted in Peter A. Howell's Foreword to *The Adelaide City Plan*. Bede was actually using that image as a metaphor for the brevity and strangeness of a human life: 'You remember, it may be, O king, that which sometimes happens in winter when you are seated at a table with your thanes. You fire is lighted, and your hall warmed, and you are inside without rain, snow, and storm. Then comes a swallow flying across the hall; he enters by one door, and leaves by another. The brief moment that he is within the hall is pleasant to him; he feels not rain nor cheerless winter weather; but the moment is brief, and he passes from winter to winter. Such, methinks, is the life of man on earth.'

5 The Rotunda

Sir Thomas Elder's letter to the council appeared as part of a general report in *The South Australian Register*, 23 August 1881, p. 1S.

Peter Morton's comment about the embarrassing state of the river pre-1880 is in *After Light*, p. 160.

The account of the opening of the Rotunda appeared in *The South Australian Advertiser*, 29 November 1882, p. 6.

The phrase 'nobly depressing rectitude' is attributed to historian Douglas Pike.

The description of the Floating Palais on the night it re-opened for its second season appeared in *The Advertiser* on 22 October 1925, p. 17.

The letter from 'Humanitas' is quoted in a longer article in *The South Australian Register*, 17 January 1845, p. 3.

Dame Roma Mitchell's duties and failings as an

air-raid warden are described in *Roma the First*, p. 84.

The account of the mine that washed ashore and killed two sailors at Beachport appears at this federal government website: http://www.ww2australia.gov.au/waratsea.lost.html.

The bizarrely complex story of the radio station closure is told by Peter Strawhan in 'The Closure of Radio 5KA, January 1941', in *Historical Studies* No. 85, 1985, pp. 550–64. Strawhan seems to think the 'code' story was a beat-up (although my Scottish grandmother, a fervent 5KA listener, was sure it was true), but his story reveals a number of violently conflicting religious, commercial and political interests.

6 The Bucket of Peaches

George Seddon's essay 'The Australian Back Yard' appears in *Australian Popular Culture*, edited by Ian Craven (Cambridge: (CUP), 1994, pp. 22–35: the quotation is from p. 22).

Hal Porter's lyrical account of Adelaide's over-productive gardens and market gardens is from the 1966 second volume of his autobiography, *The Paper Chase* (Brisbane: UQP, 1980, p. 188).

Robert Gouger reports on Colonel Light's gardening skills in *South Australia in 1837*, p. 73.

The story of Sir Thomas Playford being unable to see the point of universities comes from Bill Bryson's *Down Under* (London: Black Swan, 2001, p. 178). He doesn't say where he got it from, but he is unlikely to have been making it up.

Hugh Stretton's brisk sketch of Playford is from the 3rd edition of *Ideas For Australian Cities* (Sydney: Transit Australia Publishing, 1989, pp. 142–43). Other information on Playford comes from the general sources cited above.

George Seddon discusses Adelaide's 'Mediterraneity' or otherwise, including the comparison with Tangier and the discussion of the future of the Parklands given Adelaide's water supply, in 'Adelaide's Alter-Egos'.

The quotation from Peter Morton on the disgusting condition of 19th century Adelaide milk is from *After Light*, p. 126.

The Kaurna inscription on the sculpture at the entrance to the Festival Theatre is quoted and translated in the memoirs of Kaurna elder Uncle Lewis Yerloburka O'Brien, *And the Clock Struck Thirteen*, p. 224.

The quotation from Murray Nicol's ABC radio broadcast on Ash Wednesday is from the transcript at the ABC website: http://www.abc.net.au/

dimensions/dimensions_in_time/Transcripts/
s729955.htm, accessed 7 January 2011.

7 The Photograph

The description of Christopher Worrell as 'a bit
kinky' appeared in an article in *The Advertiser* on
Saturday, 26 May 1979 and is quoted in Anne-
Marie Mykyta's *It's A Long Way to Truro* (Melbourne:
McPhee Gribble Publishers, 1981, p. 110).

Bob O'Brien's *Young Blood: The Story of the Family
Murders* (Sydney: HarperCollins*Publishers*, 2002) is
an honest and insightful insider's account, but some
of the language and attitudes discernible in it will
prompt any reader who has not thought about this
before to give some sympathetic thought to what life
must have been like for any gay man in the South Australian police force in the 1970s and 1980s. It was
quite traumatic and damaging enough for women,
but it's clear that the homophobia of the police force
subculture in that time and place was also deeply
imbued; the drowning of George Duncan in 1972
made many of Adelaide's gay men fear for their lives,
so how any gay men in the force itself reacted can
scarcely be imagined, especially since homosexuality
had not yet been decriminalised.

Salman Rushdie's 'At the Adelaide Festival' was

first published in the *Tatler* in 1984 and reprinted in his essay collection *Imaginary Homelands: Essays and Criticism 1981–1991* (London: Granta Books in association with Penguin Books, 1991), where the quotation appears on p. 231.

The poem by 'Agnes Neale' (real name Caroline Leane) is quoted in the course of a thoughtful discussion of the 'weird Adelaide' idea by Phillip Butterss in the Preface to a collections of essays edited by him, *Southwords: Essays on Australian Writing* (Kent Town SA: Wakefield Press, 1995, p. xi).

The article headed 'Stranger Grabs Boy in Bunnings Car Park' appeared in *The Age* online on 26 January 2011, at http://www.theage.com.au/victoria/stranger-grabs-boy-in-bunnings-car-park-20110126-1a4mv.html, accessed the same day.

Barbara Hanrahan's observations about the social pages of *The Advertiser* and the liberation of the 'night self' appear in her autobiographical novel *The Scent of Eucalyptus* (London: Chatto & Windus, 1973, pp. 157–59).

All the quotations from 'Weird Adelaide' are taken from *Eight Voices of the Eighties*, where they appear on pp. 78–79.

Charles Landry is quoted in Tracy Crisp's essay 'Destination: Adelaide'.

8 The Pink Shorts

Dunstan reports his conversation with Clyde Cameron about his accent and his shoulders in *Felicia: The Political Memoirs of Don Dunstan* (Melbourne: Macmillan, 1981, p. 34) and his comments on the pink shorts also appear in *Felicia*, pp. 194–95. All other direct quotations ascribed to Dunstan are from *Felicia* unless otherwise stated.

History SA's 2008–09 travelling exhibition *Blue Jeans and Jungle Greens: Revisiting the Sixties and Seventies* featured the pink shorts. The colour photograph of them appears on the cover of *Timelines*, the Museum Historians Special Interest Group newsletter, Number 8, October 2008, and is reproduced inside to illustrate the feature article 'Pink Shorts in Parliament' by Mandy Paul of History SA, pp. 3-4. The photograph of Dunstan in his shorts on the steps of Parliament House accompanied the article 'The Surprise Pink Shorts' (no author), *The News*, 23 November 1972, p. 3.

Lyn Leader-Elliott is the former member of Dunstan's media team who tells the story of trying to keep the cameras away from the Premier in 'Interview with Lyn Leader-Elliott' (interviewer: George Lewcowicz), issue date 28 July 2010, which is part of the Don Dunstan Foundation Oral History

Project: http://dspace.flinders.edu.au/dspace/handle/2328/3208/simple-search?query=leader-elliot (pdf), accessed 4 January 2011.

The quoted newspaper article about *Lovers & Haters* is Penelope Debelle's 'Power, sex and the man in those pink shorts', *The Age*, 6 September 2007: http://www.theage.com.au/news/entertainment/power-sex-and-the-man-in-those-pink-shorts/2007/09/05/1188783313957.html, accessed 15 January 2011. The account of Vini Ciccarello's response to *Lovers and Haters* appears in 'Late South Australian premier Don Dunstan back in spotlight', by Jamie Walker, *The Australian*, 8 March 2008: http://www.theaustralian.com.au/news/dunstan-back-in-spotlight/story-e6frg6p6-1111115744222, accessed 16 January 2011. Diana Simmonds' review of *Lover and Haters* was posted on her theatre blog *Stage Noise* on 12 March 2008: http://www.stagenoise.com/reviewsdisplay.php?id=199, accessed 22 January 2011.

This chapter draws on Peter Strawhan's wonderful PhD thesis 'The importance of food and drink in the political and private life of Don Dunstan', submitted in the Discipline of History, University of Adelaide, November 2004

http://digital.library.adelaide.edu.au/dspace/
handle/2440/37726 (pdf), accessed 28 January
2011, Strawhan's thesis explores the centrality
of food and drink to Dunstan's life and beliefs,
especially in the public context of improving the
lives of South Australians and the private context
of the solace and happiness he found in cooking
for friends: 'He believed that preparing food for
friends was a wonderful way of loving them' (interview with Allan Patience, quoted on p. 309).

Dunstan's lists of his government's accom-
plishments and failures (as he saw them) during
his time in office appear in the Epilogue to *Felicia*,
pp. 315–16. Justice Michael Kirby gives his own
list of the Dunstan Labor Government's achievements in the speech he made at the NSW launch of
the Don Dunstan Foundation at the Sydney Opera
House on 28 July 1999, 'Don Dunstan's Real
Legacy': http://www.dunstan.org.au/resources/
lectures.html#Speeches, accessed 18 January 2011.

The messiness of Dunstan's cooking is described
with relish by Peter Strawhan in 'The importance
of food and drink in the political and private life
of Don Dunstan', pp. 308–09.

Hugh Stretton's description of Dunstan is from
the third edition of *Ideas For Australian Cities* (Sydney:

Transit Australia Publishing, 1989, p. 179).

The story of Playford, Dunstan and Frank Walsh in Parliament is in *Felicia*, p. 40. The photograph of Dunstan and Sir Thomas Playford together in 1972, originally published in *The Advertiser*, is reproduced in Colin Thiele's *The Adelaide Story* (Kent Town SA: Peacock Publications, 1982, p. 78). Derek Whitelock's summary description of Playford, which sounds so strangely like Dunstan as well, appears in *Adelaide From Colony to Jubilee*, p. 125. The tale of Dunstan, Playford, the government-issue pen and the official driver was told to me by my old friend and fellow Adelaidean Darcy O'Shea in private (well, semi-private; we were on Facebook) correspondence on 14 January 2011.

Dr Neal Blewett's remark about Dunstan as 'a man for all media' is quoted by Stewart Cockburn in his book *The Salisbury Affair* (Melbourne: Sun Books, 1979, p. 103), and is used by him as a chapter heading. Stewart Cockburn's 'Big Brother' objection to the media-monitoring plan is quoted in *Felicia*, p. 221.

Peter Ward's list of questions about the secret dossiers, as submitted to Dunstan on 1 September 1977, is quoted in *The Salisbury Affair*, p. 13. The story of Brigadier McKinna and Mr Justice Bray is told in *Felicia* (on p. 133) by Dunstan, who does not name names, and more recently in *Roma the First* (Kent Town SA: Wakefield Press, 2007, pp. 211–13) by Susan Magarey and Kerrie Round, who do. The story of the Police Commissioner's sacking is told in exhaustive detail from very different points of view in *The Salisbury Affair*, in *Felicia*, and in *Roma the First*. Dame Roma Mitchell, as the judge presiding over the Royal Commission into the affair, was a major figure in the story. The account of harassed citizens threatening police with 'I'll get Don Dunstan on to you' is given in *The Salisbury Affair*, pp. 108–09.

Dunstan's riposte to the press about the 'Melanesian half-caste bastard' rumours is quoted in *The Salisbury Affair*, p. 94.

Des Ryan and Mike McEwen's *It's Grossly Improper* (Adelaide: Wenan Pty Ltd, 1979) sold out immediately, and Labor lost the election that was held in September 1979, though not necessarily because of it. Peter Ward's comments about John Ceruto are quoted in *Roma the First*, p. 180.

Stories of Max Harris's school days are told at the Ern Malley website, which is written and maintained by his daughter Samela Harris: http://www.ernmalley.com/index.html, accessed 27 January 2011. The information about Dunstan's magazine and his ridicule of the Angry Penguins is in *Roma the First*, p. 156.

The story of Bonython Hall and its dance-preventing sloping floor was told by the grandson of the man who built it, the late Kym Bonython, to Susan Mitchell and recounted in her *All Things Bright and Beautiful: Murder in the City of Light* (Sydney: Pan Macmillan Australia, 2004, p. 92). Some sources dismiss this tale of dance prevention as mere Adelaide folklore, but others agree with Mitchell, who is quoting Kym Bonython in a personal conversation with her. Of course it's possible that he was having her on.

Peter Ward's comments on his own living arrangements and on Dunstan's sexuality are quoted in *Roma the First*, pp. 179 and 181 respectively. The specific gossip about Dunstan's origins also appears in *Roma the First*, pp. 154–55. Stewart Cockburn recalls his tracking down of Dunstan's birth certificate in order to investigate the 'half-caste' rumour in *The Salisbury Affair* on p. 95. The photograph of Dunstan in Fiji with his father is held by the Flinders University Library.

The article describing Dunstan's clothes at the 1972 Festival is quoted in *Roma the First*, p. 180.

The description of Dunstan's 'Nehru suit' appears in 'Interview With Lyn Leader-Elliott'.

9 The Frog Cake

Information about the history of Balfours comes from the SA Memory section of the State Library of South Australia's website, at http://www.samemory.sa.gov.au/site/page.cfm?u=370, accessed 27 March 2011, and from Balfours' own website, at http://www.balfours.com.au, accessed 27 March 2011. Information about the original Menz family business also comes from the SA Memory website, at http://www.samemory.sa.gov.au/site/page.cfm?u=1109, accessed 27 March 2011.

The story of the black and white frog cakes delivered to feed the multitudes at the Port Magpies support rally was reported in the *Portside Messenger* under the heading 'Black and white frog cakes for Magpie supporter rally', 10 February 2010, at http://www.messenger-news.whereilive.com.au/news/story/magpies-merger-deliberations-underway-at-aami, accessed 27 March 2011.

The 'frog cake stadium' April Fool's Day hoax was reported in *Adelaide Now*, the online edition of *The Advertiser*: 'Consortium hopping mad as city "frog cake"' stadium plan croaks', by Bill Ditnow,

1 April 2009, at http://www.adelaidenow.
com.au/news/frog-cake-stadium-croaks/story-
e6freo8c-1225697944913, accessed 27 March
2011.

Peter Goers' suggestion of a Big Frog Cake in
Victoria Square is made, along with many others,
in 'A Little Lunacy on Victoria Square'.

The story of the Haigh family business is told
in *The Haigh's Book of Chocolate*, by Adelaide chef and
writer Cath Kerry (Kent Town SA: Wakefield Press,
1998, pp. 18–28). This book is essential to any
collection of either cookbooks, food history books
or South Australiana; it includes history, photographs, glossaries, serving suggestions, recipes and
tips for cooking chocolate, with contributions from
Stephanie Alexander, Maggie Beer, Gay Bilson and
Bill Marchetti.

Patrick White's essay 'The Prodigal Son' was
first published in 1958 and is reprinted in *The Mac-
quarie PEN Anthology of Australian Literature* (Sydney:
Allen & Unwin, 2009, pp. 557–60).

Interviews with Cheong Liew and Philip Searle
can be found at a website commemorating the
late Melbourne restaurateur Mietta O'Donnell:
http://www.miettas.com.au/index/html, accessed
27 March 2011.

Thistle Anderson's demolition of Adelaide wine is on pp. 57–59 of *Arcadian Adelaide*.

Jane Lomax-Smith's 'great statistic' about Adelaide wine is quoted in Susan Mitchell's *All Things Bright and Beautiful: Murder in the City of Light*, p. 134.

Maggie Beer's Farm Shop website is at http://www.maggiebeer.com.au/farmshop, accessed 27 March 2011.

Susan Mitchell's memories of the Central Market are recounted in *All Things Bright and Beautiful*, p. 20.

10 The Concert Ticket

J.M. Coetzee's comments about Adelaide, made on the occasion of his becoming an Australian citizen in 2006, are quoted in 'Coetzee Takes Aust Citizenship' at *ABC Online*, 6 March 2006, at http://www.abc.net.au/news/newsitems/200603/s1585021.htm, accessed 27 March 2011.

The Paul Kelly quotation on the subject of getting out of Adelaide is from *How To Make Gravy*, p. 13.

Barbara Hanrahan's comment that in writing about Adelaide 'I might be writing about a place in a Greek myth' appears in her essay 'Earthworm Small', in *Inner Cities: Australian Women's Memory of*

Place (Melbourne: Penguin Books, 1989, p. 152), edited by Drusilla Modjeska.

Andrew Denton interviewed Antonia Banderas on *Enough Rope*, Episode 46, screened on ABC TV on 14 June 2004; the transcript is at http://www.abc.net.au/tv/enoughrope/transcripts/s1132037.htm, accessed 23 December 2010.

David Malouf's essay 'The Happy Life: The Search for Contentment in the Modern World' was published in Black Inc's *Quarterly Essay* series, Issue 41 (2011). The quotation comes from pp. 54–55.

All reasonable efforts were taken to obtain permission to use copyright material reproduced in this book, but in some cases copyright holders could not be traced. The author welcomes information in this regard.

Thanks to Phillipa McGuinness for giving me the opportunity to write this book, and so to learn more about my city. Thanks also to my editor, Sarah Shrubb, who has been a model of patience, skill and good humour in identifying problems and persuading me to fix them.

Thanks also for information and generous

help to Dr Christine Garnaut of the School of Art, Architecture and Design at the University of South Australia; to Triss Roberts from the Queen Adelaide Society; to the staff of the University of Adelaide Library, particularly in Rare Books; and to the staff of the Art Gallery of South Australia, especially Jin Whittington, Sue Smith, Georgia Hale and Tracey Lock-Weir.

Thanks to the various people from whom I received support, encouragement, inspiration and/ or help: Phil Broderick, Phil Butterss, Delia Falconer, Leonie Hale, Greg Mackie, Lyn McCredden, Darcy O'Shea, Christopher Pearson, Paul Salzman, Jared Thomas and Stephanie Trigg. Thanks generally to my family and friends, for tolerating my neglect, and more specifically to Robyn Groves for the helpful feedback and the magical writing robe; to my father, Colin Goldsworthy, for sharing his memories of Adelaide; and to Deej Eszenyi and Marion Byrne for giving me new things to think about and patiently enduring hours of unsolicited instruction over Saturday morning coffee in obscure points of South Australian social history.

Thanks most of all, for their unfailing enthusiasm and loving support, to Robyn, to my dad, and to the Dark Man.